THE POWER

OF

MENTORING

WingSpread Publishers
Chicago, Illinois

www.moodypublishers.com

An imprint of Moody Publishers

MARTIN SANDERS

THE POWER OF MENTORING

SHAPING PEOPLE WHO WILL

SHAPE THE WORLD

WingSpread Publishers

Chicago, Illinois

To
Dr. Leighton Ford,
friend, mentor, coach and more.

To
Dianna
Your amazing hospitality over the years
has created an idyllic environment for hundreds
to tell their personal stories in our home.
Thanks for pulling together ten years of writing
to see this book become reality.
It would not have happened without you.

Table of Contents

Foreword

FOR THE PAST TWO decades, my own ministry has focused on identifying, mentoring and developing the emerging young leaders in the Body of Christ worldwide. Again and again I have found that what they most want is a senior leader who will walk with them and be a wise guide to them—but too often there are not enough mentors to meet the need.

I have also frequently been asked to recommend books on the ministry of mentoring and have been hard-pressed to come up with really good ones—and practical ones. That is why I am now pleased to tell about Martin Sanders' *The Power of Mentoring*. For some years I have been urging Martin to put his teaching and insights into print, so I am grateful that he has done so in this valuable book. It is rich in content—broad in its coverage, deep in its understanding of relationships, useful in its suggestions, wise out of Martin's own experiences in mentoring—and passionate at its heart. I hope it will be widely read and put into practice even more.

It is important for readers to know that Martin Sanders practices what he teaches. I have known Martin for over a decade, from the time he applied to be a part of the Arrow Leadership Program. Frankly, at the time I wondered why someone who was already a seminary professor would want to be part of a development program for young leaders, since he himself already was a well-known leader. I assumed that he wanted to observe and get ideas that he could take back home.

Over the course of the program, Martin proved to be a very teacheable teacher! He not only took part in every session, but he did it with grace and humility, not trying to impress anyone with his experience and credentials, but simply participating as a member of the group. I noticed how the other young leaders in the program were drawn to Martin and the care with which he related to them. He was truly a shepherd of shepherds.

Since then, Martin and I have become close friends, and I have followed his ministry with interest and joy. He is part of the international Point Group of leaders of his generation with which I meet every year, and it has been tremendously encouraging to see the growth of his ministry in scope and depth and how he has been warmly embraced as a brother and a leader by these men and women from around the world.

Martin also is one of the key teachers for our Sandy Ford retreats, in which each year we bring together outstanding seminary students and provide them with scholarship help for their studies and teach them on the topics of leadership and evangelism. In these situations, Martin excels at the front of the classroom—but my most lasting memories of him are of the times when he sits by the hour with student after student, listening carefully to them and speaking wisdom and truth into their lives.

The savor of Christ flows from Martin's life and can be sensed in this fine book. I warmly commend it, and I pray that in the reading of it many will be called both to find mentors and also to mentor others.

Leighton Ford, president
Leighton Ford Ministries
Charlotte, North Carolina

Preface

AS A GRADUATE STUDENT, I began my pastoral ministry in 1980. The philosophy I espoused then was simply this: "Discipleship is the ministry under which the entire Church is to function!" It seemed very clear to me: Jesus began His ministry by calling disciples; He discipled those disciples; His final instruction to those disciples was to make more disciples, who would make more disciples, to the ends of the earth. It was clear. It was simple. It was straightforward. Why do anything else?

I set up discipleship frameworks for new believers, for cell groups, for developing leaders and for older leaders to mentor emerging leaders. It seemed clear and simple. Results happened quickly. I was asked to assist other churches in creating these useful structures, and I remember thinking then, *Why does this seem so innovative or creative to other people?*

Over the years, the same material and simple structures have been used to help hundreds of churches develop that discipleship umbrella. Now, twenty-four years after those initial experiences, it is amazing to me how fresh, even "innovative," that material remains in many church circles.

For so many of the emerging young leaders around the world the quest for a mentor moves well beyond a wishful desire; it is a longing and an actual developmental need. So many of them did not receive the necessary personal, emotional or developmental building blocks of character, confidence and courage that are required to create effective leadership qualities. The longing for a mentor is one tangible expression of a desire to fill that need. This longing is repeatedly expressed in conferences on every continent by hundreds of gifted young leaders. It is hard to overstate the need for mentoring!

The concept for this book began thirteen years ago in conversations that I had with Paul Bubna, past president of The Christian and Missionary Alliance. We began the writing process together, but his wife's illness and premature death halted our progress. Eight years ago, we picked up the challenge again, but Paul's life suddenly ended as well, and the writing again came to a halt. Now, finally completed, *The Power of Mentoring* is designed to address some of the issues that Paul and I discussed in our early conversations about the need for mentoring.

The material in this book comes from nearly twenty-five years of ministry in churches, from work in seminaries and graduate schools in ten countries and from experience with seminars, conferences and mentoring networks developed in some forty countries. It is a response to the two key questions I am asked regularly: "How can I find a mentor?" and "I have been asked to mentor someone; what do I do?" It is designed to provide insight and structures, motivation and confidence, philosophy and skills, inspiration and implementation strategies for you and your journey through mentoring. We will move through the basics of spiritual and character formation to structures for mentoring the next generation of leaders. It is both a natural and an intentional progression.

What will it take for the churches who clearly long to follow the teachings of Jesus to implement His mission to simply make disciples who are able and willing to make more disciples? I believe that mentoring is the answer. It really is time to get this one right! The need for mentoring is unbelievably high. The availability of able and willing mentors in most countries of the world is incredibly low. My hope is that this book can change that.

Acknowledgments

I OWE MUCH TO the many who have contributed to the development of this book.

To the developmental mentors of my life: my father; Leighton Ford; Carl Sovine; Bobby Clinton; Royal Bailey; and Paul Bubna. You all played key roles in my development.

To the churches I have served: Wesley Church, Waukegan, IL; Glen Cairn Church, Regina, Saskatchewan; and Our Redeemer, Elgin, IL.

To the discipleship and mentoring group participants, especially the Eagles Group: Doug Bender; Steve Harper; David King; Warren Reeve; Jonathan Schaeffer; Jeff Singfiel; Joel Smith; and Mike Sohm. You are a great bunch of leaders.

To the Alliance Theological Seminary community and administration. Thanks for the sabbatical.

To the writing and research assistants: Sally Mondary; Shirley Hyun; Sam Park; and Dean Groetzinger. A special thank you to Anita Hartzfeld Alvarez.

To the generous friends in Florida who provided vehicles and places on the water for writing: the Sorensens and the Jahnas.

To the leadership of Ken Paton and Doug Wicks. I remember the meeting at the Newark Airport Marriott!

1

Mentoring and the Developmental Process

The Development of Character

AS A YOUNG PASTOR, I was dismayed at my lack of effectiveness and my inability to see God's power working in my life and ministry. I decided to take at least a year to study the Scriptures and observe manifestations of God's power in the Bible. I would analyze each of them and uncover principles or insights that could help me. As I finished my preliminary evaluations of the study and began to look for patterns, I discovered that the kind of people God used significantly were those whose character conformed to Christ's.

Although this insight in itself is not very profound, at the time it was profound for me because I had been looking for a magic formula that would help me see more results in my life and ministry. I found that the secret had to do with issues of the heart and character. In Romans 8:29, we are promised that as children of God we are predestined to conform to the image of Christ. God's primary purpose and passion is for us to take on His character and reflect His grace. No matter how much we may excel in any aspect of life, no matter how much success we attain and no matter how effective we are perceived to be, the "success" we reach for in life will ultimately be limited without character development.

I also discovered that in a successful ministry there is often a revelation of God's power in a dramatic way, in addition to people taking risks and putting their faith on the edge (which can also put it on the edge of disaster). People of character and integrity who take risks are most often the kind of people who see God's power and the fullness of His blessing upon their lives and ministries.

I have learned much more about this as the years have gone by, but I repeatedly go back to the simplicity of this understanding: It is heart, character and integrity, trusting God beyond my own ability and risking faith that really demonstrate His power. Ministry in general and mentoring in particular can be summarized in this same way. As emerging leaders are mentored through stages of personal, spiritual and emotional development, character formation takes center stage. It is the primary component and a constant in the mentoring and developmental processes. If we can follow the pattern set out in the Bible and focus on character formation, God can use it in our lives and ministries. We will be receptacles for Christ's character and power.

Developing the Person in Ministry

Individuals move through stages of life development at many different paces. The order of the stages is far more predictable, however. The following figure, created by Paul Stanley, shows the lifelong developmental phases through three general stages of life.

Lifelong Developmental Process[1]		
Birth-18--------18-30------------ 30-50------------- 50+-----		
Age of Learning	Age of Contribution	Age of Investment
Who am I?	What do I do?	Invest in whom/what?

Stanley's chart helps us identify the changes of focus and perspective that a person needs as he or she progresses through the stages. The "Age of Learning," from ages eighteen to thirty, focuses on being "unbusy," enjoying new experiences, gaining perspective and having a mentor or coach to help in the process. In the "Age of Contribution," from ages thirty to fifty, the focus moves to clarifying all the experiences of one's life to avoid becoming unfocused and reaching a plateau. The goal is to sharpen one's life message or goal for purposes of maximum impact. Peers as well as a mentor will aid in this process. The "Age of Investment," from ages fifty and older, focuses on leaving a lasting legacy and passing on the passions that have driven one's life. At this point, peer mentors are crucial for keeping focus and perspective.

Mentoring is viewed as the facilitation of the lifelong developmental process whereby individuals move through various stages of human, emotional, spiritual, educational, intellectual and other aspects of development. With this view, we can then work with the "big picture" of the formative process rather than getting lost or stuck in one particular aspect or stage of mentoring.

Perspective

In any given week, I receive several phone calls from young leaders who have "perspective" questions. Sometimes the questions are theological, other times they are about personal perspectives on a particular topic, and still other questions are about trends, histories, etc. The emerging leader often ends the conversation with a word of appreciation and a statement about how challenging it is to get perspective.

Throughout the mentoring process it is common for a mentoree to ask for perspective. Sometimes the perspective is historic, subcultural, a local or regional issue or maybe even a theological reflection. The mentoree becomes keenly aware that the mentor has both experience and wisdom that can prove helpful. The process is most effective when the mentor offers insights, reflections and perspective rather than answering the question and settling the issue. It is true that good questions don't lead to answers but to more questions.

Key Questions

Within the mentoring relationship, key questions are crucial to helping guide the mentoree in life direction and character development. These are questions that help the mentoree reflect on reasons behind personal issues or behaviors or establish personal guidelines for dealing with a particular issue. By exploring these issues, the root of the problem is attacked and resolved. This is the opposite of superficially mending the outer layer of the "mental" skin that the outside world sees and which inevitably tears in a time of crisis. By asking good questions and listening, and through effective feedback (both reflective and directive), the mentor aids the emerging leader with perspective and life development.

Coaching

After more than a decade of teaching pastoral theology in seminaries, I discovered a consistent pattern in student papers: They tended to focus more on behavior than on life direction. Several times each semester I would receive a paper from a well-intentioned student who had included some thought such as, "If I could only clean up my life. If I could only get rid of this be-setting sin or this unresolved issue. If I could only be *holy enough,* then I would see God really at work in my life. Then I would be more effective for the cause of Christ and the kingdom of God." These students think that if they could just get past one particular issue (usually one that seems most significant at the time), if they could only lead a life that was more holy, then they would see more of God's power.

Mentoring is the facilitation of the lifelong development process whereby individuals move through various stages of human, emotional, spiritual, educational and intellectual development.

Over the past several decades the emphasis throughout North America, both in society at large as well as in the Church, has been on the development of cognitive understanding and behaviorism. The general consensus has been that if a person modifies undesirable behavior, thinks the right thoughts and creates a healthy environment in which he or she makes good decisions, he or she will be developing effectively. In simpler terms, if a person thinks the right thoughts and does the right "stuff," he or she will develop effectively. Therefore, in theory, this formula *should* develop the right kind of person. But behaviorism has often failed to produce balanced, healthy leaders, and what is missing is related to issues of character.

This is where the mentoring process can be used to facilitate the mentoree's direction in life and the formation of character that will produce an effective individual. While behaviorism changes people from the outside in, the mentoring process picks up where behaviorism fails because in mentoring, people are changed from the inside out. It should focus more on *coaching* in life direction rather than on *modifying behavior* or *changing thought processes*. Since the mentoring process consists of forming the overall person, and character development in particular, it will be more useful to focus on facilitating the individual as he or she moves through the stages of development rather than concentrating primarily on behaviors, cognitive development or even skill acquisition.

It is important for the emerging leader to understand that issues related to personal and character development will not change quickly or be alleviated with some form of behavior modification. Changes will occur over time, with prayer and reflection, obedience and faithfulness, and often with more than one attempt. What is really important is the formation of character, walking with God over the long run and understanding His grace and forgiveness. *This* is the formation of godly character whereby one becomes the effective servant God can and does use.

The Power of Permission

Within many organizations, including the Church, there is often a subtle (and sometimes not so subtle) pressure to conform to established guidelines and expectations, whether they are admitted and known to all or disguised and left to be discerned by the individual. They range from glass ceilings to age and education requirements, from attire to patterns of speech, from theological positions to political preferences. Some are blatant while others are masterfully disguised. But underneath each is the pressure to conform. These pressures can be overwhelmingly stifling to an individual's growth.

The power of permission may be one of the single most significant things a mentor can offer to a mentoree. It may be permission to fail or even to succeed wildly. It may be permission to work outside the general consensus or guidelines. It may be permission to be more passionate than controlled. It may be permission to work fewer hours in the office in order to pursue one of the personal development issues that the mentoree is currently facing.

The other side of permission involves the mentor allowing the mentoree to explore his or her motives, drive and passions and giving permission for the mentoree to be healthy, effective and faithful, but not necessarily amazing at any particular stage of his or her personal development.

One highly motivated young pastor told me of the time he took a course for personal development. As he finished penning a paper in which he articulated all of his goals, dreams and visions (in his mind, masterfully articulating what his life and ministry were going to look like), the professor gave him a few words of wisdom that changed the course of his life: "You have articulated everything well. It is an 'A' paper. But what would happen if you weren't 'super'? What if you did not become this amazing person? What would be wrong with simply being faithful and effective and enjoying your life, faith and ministry? Why do you have to be 'super'?"

The young pastor said that these remarks forced him to do a lot of deep reflection on some things he really did not want to think about. But he began asking himself, "So what if I am not 'super'?" He admitted that while reflecting on his life he discovered that he had never been *great* at anything. He was a good athlete, but not great. He had been a B+ student who had had to work hard to get some A's. He realized that he was never amazing. That same day he made a decision to work less and think more. He decided to focus less on success and being "super" and to enjoy his life, family and ministry more. He said that the result, to his surprise, was that not only was life far more enjoyable, but he was far more effective at everything he did. By trying less he actually succeeded more.

The words spoken by his professor were words of permission. Speak those words of permission to the next generation of emerging leaders so they can explore their gifts and strengths, so they can have less pressure to be "great" and more energy to focus on what God has given them in order to become effective leaders.

The Power of Intentional Development

A colleague of mine once told me a story of a time when he was a presenter at a conference. To his surprise, he discovered that one of his former college professors was also presenting. The first morning they met together for breakfast. They reminisced and caught up on some acquaintances they both knew. As the conversation began to naturally wind down, the former professor said, "It really is hard to know when students graduate how they are going to end up, isn't it?" They grew silent while they continued to eat their breakfast. After a while it seemed like the professor had something to say. He nervously tugged at his tie, stretched his neck, stammered a bit and then said, "Frankly, you have been a surprise to all of us." My colleague responded, "What, did you peg me for a loser?" The professor said, "Not at all. But no one had any idea that you would develop as rapidly as you have and go as far as you did. It's been great to see. But, frankly, it's been a surprise to everyone."

As emerging leaders are mentored through stages of development, character formation takes center stage. It is the primary component and a constant in mentoring.

When observing emerging leaders, whether they are interns, recent college graduates, seminary students, ministerial hopefuls or evangelist wannabes, it is nearly impossible to predict who will be highly effective, who will be faithful to his or her calling, marriage or church and who will finish well. Two key indicators that seem to point people to a successful end in the development of life, faithfulness and effectiveness are: 1) the lifelong pursuit of character formation throughout the various stages of life; and 2) the presence of a mentor(s) to guide them.

My colleague and his professor came back to this conversation more than one time during the conference. From the professor's perspective, the reasons behind my colleague's development, both in its quality and pace, centered around intentional development—intentionally pursuing and taking an active role in one's development—and character development. This book will analyze and discuss the principles of *intentional development* and *character development* that enable young leaders to be effective in their lives and their ministries. We will also recount the power of the mentoring relationship in relation to the developmental process.

Key Thoughts from This Chapter

1. Character development is the key to effective mentoring and leadership development.
2. There are three key stages to life development:
   a. The Age of Learning, Ages 18-30
   b. The Age of Contribution, Ages 30-50
   c. The Age of Investment, Age 50 and older
3. Mentoring involves:
   a. Providing perspective
   b. Asking key questions
   c. A focus on coaching rather than behavior modification
4. The power of permission that is given from mentor to mentoree involves:
   a. Permission to succeed and fail
   b. Permission to try new things
   c. Permission to be different and not conform

d. Permission to not be amazing, but to pursue excellence

Questions for Further Reflection

1. Since a primary key of mentoring is character development, what aspect of character formation needs to be developed in your life at this time?
2. Where do you see yourself in the stages of life development? Are you comfortable with your character development, the areas in which you've invested your life and your potential legacy at this time in your life?
3. Regardless of your age, as you look toward your next stage of development, will your focus be more on the character, emotional, spiritual or simply human dimension of your life?

Action Plan

1. Identify yourself by age and season of life. What are two things that clearly represent you at this time?
2. Begin to identify your two greatest mentoring needs or desires.

Note

1. *Mentor Training Seminar Manual*. Charlotte: Leighton Ford Ministries, 1996. Used with permission from Arrow Leadership Ministries, www.arrowleadership.org.

2
A Rationale for Mentoring

THROUGHOUT THE LAST CENTURY the Western world has seen its share of fads of all kinds, from toys to fashion, and the Church has not been exempt from these trends. Some have left a positive impact on us, and others were not quite as positive. As a result, when the topic of mentoring comes up, some people think that it's just one of the latest fads to capture the attention of church leaders who are looking for a quick fix for greater effectiveness.

Mentoring, however, is not simply the most recent trend to emerge on the North American church scene. The concept of mentoring is rooted in our past, and it is at the very core of how the next generation of leaders is developed. As focus is given to the intentional development of purposeful relationships between emerging leaders and established leaders, the developmental interactions that take place bring greater effectiveness to both groups of individuals. In many ways, the future health of the Church depends upon these mentoring relationships.

Passing on the Torch

One of the key realities of life and faith is that each generation is required to hand over the reins to the next generation of leaders. It was true when Moses passed the torch to Joshua. It was true when Paul passed the torch to Timothy. It is true now and will continue to be so. Since this is the case, why not plan to do it systematically? Why not plan it and carry it out with purposeful intentionality? Why not purposefully groom the next generation so that they feel confident? It makes sense, right? Then why doesn't it already work this way?

At a mentoring conference in Anaheim, California, some 350 leaders, mostly in their fifties and sixties, gathered to share ideas and resources for effective mentoring in the Church. As the youngest on a team of seven presenters at the conference, I was the only person in the entire group who was in his thirties (and there were probably only a handful in their forties). As the conference went on, it became quite clear that there was some hesitation, and even resentment, about passing on leadership to the next generation. It seemed appropriate for me to address this issue, as I was the youngest person in the group.

Late on the second afternoon, I stood in front of the group dressed unlike everyone else (I was the only male with a ponytail) and clearly not representing what most would think of as the best of what the future of the Church should look like. I said to the group, "The prospect of having to pass on the leadership of your ministry, your church and even your denomination to people who look like me both scares and annoys many of you. Whether you admit it or not, you have a measuring stick that you use, and you come alongside emerging leaders like me and hold it up. You calculate issues of holiness, spirituality, credibility and other things you hold in high regard. And often, without even talking to me or my peers, you analyze us, critique us and pass judgment upon us. Whether you admit it or not, you do it, and we know it.

"I want to say to you honestly today, you're right. I don't measure up in a number of things so many of you are strong in. I need more development in leading a holy life. I wish my prayer life was more effective and consistent. I wish a number of things in my life were further developed. But I don't need you to critique me and tell me how far I've fallen short from your perspective. I need you to coach me. I need you to show me how to be in a leadership position and, God willing, continue in a leadership position. Like it or not, you will turn the future of your ministry over to someone, and probably to someone like me. It's not a very pleasant thought, is it? But rather than evaluating and critiquing me, mentor me. Spend *time* with me. *Show* me. *Teach* me what you know. *Help* me to be a man of wisdom and to love God the way you do. I want it. The Church needs it. The future health of the Church depends on it. Don't critique me. *Mentor* me!"

It got really quiet in the auditorium. At the end of the session, a line of more than sixty people gathered in front of me. People wanted to talk with me, pray with me and seek forgiveness from me. People I'd never met before said, "You're so right. I have done that and I'm sorry." The outcome of that conference has been encouraging to me as a member of the middle generation of leaders. I've seen that the older generation of established leaders, at least some of them, have begun to catch the vision of what can happen if they intentionally mentor people they don't necessarily approve of but who have a bonded purpose in the mission of Christ and His Church. Intentionally mentoring the next generation will ensure that the work of God that began in us—the work of His kingdom—will continue past our own lifetime.

Historic Perspective

The concept of mentoring has significant historic roots. At its most basic core is the concept of apprenticeship. In an apprenticeship, the young apprentice connected, even attached, himself to an established "master" in a particular field. The role of the master was to teach the apprentice the art of the master's particular trade. The role of the apprentice was to learn not only the function of the trade but the nuances and details that made the master the *master*. The practice has a long and rich tradition of producing both functional and even world-class masters out of young, emerging apprentices.

The limitation of an apprenticeship was that the effectiveness lasted only as long as the master was in control. The relationship was typically severed when the apprentice matched the master's skill. The apprentice was then considered competition. In the mentoring relationship, however, the role of the mentor from the very inception is to help the mentoree reach his or her fullest potential, which can mean that the mentoree may surpass the mentor at some point. Thus, the mentoring process is not as much about the mentor as it is about the current and future development of the mentoree.

A Clear and Present Need

I am often asked by older leaders, "Why do younger leaders feel such a need to be mentored? No one mentored us, and we did fine. Didn't we?"

It is evident that our society has changed since World War II at a rate that has not been seen at any other time in recorded history. In the last thirty years of the twentieth century, the rate of change seems to have accelerated even more. Although older and established leaders will acknowledge this, many do not take the time to process the fact that all of these changes have created very different kinds of people with uniquely different needs and perspectives.

> One of the key realities of life and faith is that each generation is required to hand over the reins to the next generation of leaders. Since this is the case, why not plan to do it systematically?

In an analysis of the cultural changes within North America over the last thirty years, five factors emerge that contribute in some way to the rising need for intentional mentoring within our current cultural context:

1. *Loss of heroes.* Throughout the last decade or more, nearly every major periodical in the United States and Canada has done a cover story on the absence of heroes and role models and the impact that it has on society in general and on the emerging generations in particular.

2. *Loss of "common sense."* In the first six decades of the twentieth century within North America

there existed a body of knowledge and a shared value simply referred to as "common sense." Increasingly, by the end of the twentieth century and the emerging years of the twenty-first century, this shared value began to disappear. The lack of this shared knowledge often necessitates the development of a common language in the mentoring relationship, as well as increases the need for mentors to provide perspective and explain simply why some things are the way they are, both in organizations and in relationships.

3. *Societal mobility.* In every young leaders' conference at which I speak, I ask how many of the attendees live within a 100-mile radius of where they grew up. Often no one raises a hand. At best, only a quarter of them respond. When a young leader no longer has immediate access to people, places or institutions that he or she has known, the desire and need for mentoring increases.

4. *MTV: visual orientation; "show me how."* A person who grows up watching music videos becomes a significantly different person than someone who grew up listening to music. Someone who grew up listening to music might hear a favorite song that triggers memories of a particular time in his or her life, including the geographic location, clothing, car, friends, etc. This brings about a time of reflection on the person's life. Someone who grew up watching music might hear a favorite song and instead recall

images from the music video. Because the images have already been provided for that person, it is challenging for him or her to reflect very deeply—or at all—on his or her life.

5. *Postponed maturity*. With the changes occurring in North American society, perceptions of time and age are changing as well. In the 1960s the saying went, "You can't trust anyone over thirty." Then women's magazines announced that forty was the new thirty. Now, as Baby Boomers are aging, fifty has become the new forty. Fifteen to twenty years ago young leaders' programs focused on people primarily in their twenties and early thirties. Now, it is common for them to extend to age forty, with many requests for admission coming from people up to forty-five years old. Postponed maturity increases the need as well as the desire for mentoring.

Although none of the above issues alone is a major one, the combination of these factors makes for a uniquely different context than established leaders knew in their time of development. Emerging leaders today grew up in a uniquely different context than leaders who are in their fifties and sixties. Because today's emerging leaders lack familial stability, a mutual cultural morality and frameworks to work within, the individuals *themselves* are uniquely different people with very different needs, values, perspectives and ideas. The goal of mentoring is to create intentional relationships that aid the individual mentoree in developing his or her own effectiveness by filling the needs that the above issues have caused in our society.

Coaching the Individual

In the mentoring context, each individual will have one significant mentor, or even several resource people, to help him or her reach optimum effectiveness. Although the mentor's role is uniquely different from each of the following, there is a bit of each included: coach, spiritual guide, parent, counselor and trusted friend.

One of the best analogies of the role of a mentor is found in professional baseball. In major league baseball, every team has a batting coach whose job is to watch each player individually as he bats and tell him what he's doing right or wrong. It's intriguing to note that the players are often paid more—sometimes ten or twenty times more—than the coach. Even multimillion-dollar players need someone to stand there, hour after hour, and watch them bat. The coach says things like: "You're dropping your elbow too soon." "You're stepping with your left foot too quickly." "It might be good to move back in the batter's box just a little." "When this particular kind of pitch comes, time your swing just a split second earlier."

The players need the coach to help them not to *hit* the ball, but to hit the ball *better*, to hit it *farther*, to hit it *more often*. The coach may have never been as good a hitter as the player that he is coaching, but he's learned from experience, from watching thousands of players and by watching the game over the course of his life. He is, in essence, a master at the nuances of the game, especially hitting.

The parallels to mentoring are so clear. What many emerging leaders need is someone to be with them to watch and say, "Consider this." "Think about this." "Did you ever notice that when this happens you respond this way?" They need a coach who asks questions, gives more than advice and helps his or her mentorees to reflect on how to do something just a bit better. For mentorees to reach their greatest potential, it takes a mentor to ask key questions, give a few pointers, be there at key moments, be a trusted friend and *listen*.

The Wisdom of the Ages

As a young leader, I was fortunate to have many opportunities to learn from older leaders. These people have many descriptors: seasoned veterans, gifted leaders, masters of the art, women of prayer, men of wisdom, people of humility, women and men who walked with God, people of prophetic wisdom, insight and discernment, humble servants. Whatever the descriptor, each one has passed on to me a significant amount of insight for personal development. Their influence upon me has been monumental. Most of the time I have had to ask, pursue and at times insist in order to have them as mentors and receive what I wanted and needed from them. Very few have offered.

These established leaders are hesitant because they don't always understand the values and approaches of the younger generations. Also, our culture does not value the aged or their wisdom, and therefore these older leaders do not see themselves or their experiences as something that the younger generations seek. Due to our society's lack of appreciation for age, experience and wisdom, many older adults have not thought through the process of passing on what they have learned in a transferable, tangible way.

Some feel they lack the time to mentor, some feel they have nothing to offer, some have too many other commitments and others fear they will not meet all of the expectations. The reasons are many, but these leaders are sorely needed as mentors!

I was in my late thirties when I attended a national denominational conference, and in the midst of that conference I had an incredible awakening. It became really clear to me that I was no longer one of the "sharp, young guys" there. This became so clear because the sharp, young guys were coming to me with questions— mentoring questions! They clearly viewed me as one of the "older guys"! I must admit that for a little while I had a minor identity crisis. *Oh, no, I'm not one of the sharp, young guys anymore. What will I do now?*

> The role of the mentor from the very inception is to help the mentoree reach his or her fullest potential.

So I took some time one afternoon to go for a walk and to think and reflect. I thought to myself, *It's OK. I've had a good run, a pretty long run, of being one of the sharp, young guys. I had some recognition and some influence beyond my local church in my mid-twenties, had the chance to travel and speak widely and consult in a wide variety of places.* As the self talk continued I said to myself, *It's OK; it's time. I've had a good run, and now it's time to make the transition to becoming one of the seasoned veterans who's there as a coach, mentor and resource person for the really sharp, young men and women in ministry.* At the end of the afternoon I felt pretty good about it and looked at it as the next developmental stage of my mission—I was now a seasoned veteran entering the middle years of life and ministry.

I quickly fast-forwarded and wondered, *But what comes after this?* And with growing excitement I thought, *If I do this stage well, stay current, read widely and keep sharp, it won't be long before I can become a sage! A man of wisdom!* I thought, *Oh, this will be cool. Instead of a ponytail, I'll do the shaved-head thing with a nice goatee. And as a sage you don't have to say much. People come and want to talk and ask you questions, and you mostly just make noises: "Mmmm." "Oooh." "Yes." "Trust God." "Let me pray."*

I had a little fun with this imagery, but it really did register for me that it was natural to move out of the "sharp, young guy" stage. It's natural to move into the role of the seasoned veteran who becomes a coach and a resource person. But I also prayed and said, "God, can I develop well so that I might have the heart, mind and character to become a man of wisdom?"

We need the wisdom and experiences of our elders to help us form our character and frame our development. We need our mentors to reframe our experiences, failures and frustrations into principles and to be willing to share them in relational frameworks. Their wisdom is so valuable and cannot be found in any other substitute. Let's take advantage of the wisdom God has given leaders throughout the ages and use it for our growth. We need them in the Church. May God show us how to become women and men of wisdom who will pass that wisdom on to the next generation, and the next and the next.

Key Thoughts from This Chapter

1. Mentoring is a relational experience that empowers the emerging leader; in the apprentice model the master often kept control and was unable to empower the younger person.
2. The rising need for mentoring in North America is due to:
   a. Loss of heroes
   b. Loss of "common sense"
   c. Societal mobility
   d. MTV: visual orientation; "show me how"
   e. Postponed maturity
3. The mentor is like the batting coach in major league baseball. He or she becomes a student of the mentoree's life, asking strategic questions and offering insights to help the mentoree be more effective.

Questions for Further Reflection

1. Take time to specifically describe your mentoring desires and needs. Who are the best two people to assist you in addressing these?
2. What is the best context or relationship in which to have those needs met?
3. What do you have to offer the next generation of emerging leaders? Identify strengths, areas of brokenness, skills, etc.

Action Plan

1. Begin to determine the type of wisdom an older leader could offer to you that would benefit you the most.

3

Developing Meaningful Relationships

I ONCE SPOKE AT a seminar at a large church in Brooklyn on the topic "Developing Men of Godly Character." I was to speak about developing one's personal character and how that carried over into relationships. I spent the first hour of my session on what it means to be a man of character and integrity. In the last forty-five minutes I explained what it means to have healthy relationships, focusing particularly on intimacy, what it looks and feels like and how it works out in relationships with other men, women and God.

As I finished my seminar, it was clear that the material had made a significant impact on the 500 men who were there. We had a short question-and-answer time afterward, and then I pronounced a blessing upon them. I asked that the Spirit of God would empower them to become men of real character and integrity in their lives and relationships.

I was not prepared for the response that followed. More than fifty men immediately formed a line to talk to me, and as others gathered to talk in small groups, the line continued to grow. The men responded to the seminar in three general ways. The first was, "I have never, ever heard a real man talk about this stuff. How did you learn this?" The second was, "Where can I find men who know this who I can learn from?" The third took on a tone of intimidation: "Who do you think you are? Who are you to say this?" The implication was that I was outside the community, the culture and the racial subculture. (I'm not sure if I was the only Caucasian at the conference, but I was that day.) But I didn't back down to those negative responses. I looked the men in the eye and asked them to describe what was behind their anger and attempts at intimidation. What response were they looking for? These men ultimately changed their responses when they saw that their approach wasn't going to work. Then, genuine questions of the heart began to come from them as well.

I walked away from the conference that day saying, "God, will You raise up leaders, mentors, even a whole generation of men, who will understand intimacy, talk about it and model real intimacy for the next generation of men?" I had a growing awareness that that day might impact generations to come more than any other teaching I could have presented.

Developing Significant Relationships

At the very heart of mentoring are the significant relationships that develop within that process. An important part of cultivating young leaders involves broadening their experiences with healthy relationships that are mutual, developmental and purposeful, and that often remain close for years.

Developing a healthy mentoring relationship involves asking key questions and then listening. In most cases it is more of a reflective process than a telling one. Unfortunately, many young women and men report that their mentors spend most of their time talking, lecturing and even preaching *to* them. The intimate atmosphere that surrounds these relationships can be threatening for mentors who do better as "the boss," the answer person or the one in charge. This kind of mentor usually feels more comfortable giving information than sharing life and experiences. In denominations where mentoring programs have been structured through the districts or regions and older pastors are selected or assigned, a common report from the protégé goes like this: "We meet for a few hours once a month or so, and he talks about his agenda, his issues, the things he's thinking about." In this scenario, the mentor is merely giving out information—much like a sage would. The protégé often feels like there's no room to ask questions, to pray together, to build the relationship, and little time for the things that are important to him or her. A mentor needs to be vulnerable, to share his or her life and experiences and to listen and elicit information from the mentoree.

Throughout this book there will be little or no distinction made between women and men as we discuss the mentoring process. When it comes to relationships, however, men often need more direct coaching on what healthy friendships look like, especially as they move out of high school and college and into adulthood. Therefore, in this chapter, I would like to focus on the issue of men and friendships.

Men and Friendships

Many men spend little time thinking about friendships. Up through their midlife years, men tend to focus on career, work, tasks and the functional aspects of life. When they do think about friendships, they admit that they are disappointed in their relationships with other men. Stuart Miller says,

> Men may have wives, they may even have other women friends, but their relationships with other men . . . are generally characterized by thinness, insincerity, and even chronic wariness.[1]

This seems to be true of many North American men.

The Bible gives us a number of examples of healthy male relationships and friendships. In *The Friendless American Male*, David W. Smith outlines six principles of friendship taken from Scripture:

> Principle 1: GOD-CENTERED—unifying the relationship on a common faith (Psalm 1)
>
> Principle 2: FORMATION OF COVENANT—expressing commitment to each other through a symbolic gesture (1 Samuel 18:3)
>
> Principle 3: FAITHFULNESS—building trust and dependability (Proverbs 18:24)
>
> Principle 4: SOCIAL INVOLVEMENT—reaching out to others by the investment of time and concern (Proverbs 14:21)
>
> Principle 5: CANDOR—helping friends face the truth, providing perspective and aiding in making wise decisions (Proverbs 17:10)
>
> Principle 6: RESPECT—showing esteem for, honor to and consideration for the humanness of each other (Proverbs 25:17)[2]

These general guidelines from Scripture highlight the theme of friendship for both genders. Yet many men confess that they have never had these types of relationships, nor do they know how to develop them.

For mentoring relationships to be effective, there are several steps men need to follow. First, they must identify their need for friendships and relationships with other men. Next, they should begin developing relational skills to use in friendships. Then, they can move into the more meaningful implications of communicating deeper aspects of their lives.

> Developing a healthy mentoring relationship
> involves asking key questions and then
> listening. It is far more a reflective process
> than telling, lecturing or preaching.

Creating contexts that make this process easier is a helpful way to start. We often begin mentoring groups, seminars or conferences at a professional athletic event, on an outdoor wilderness activity (hiking, whitewater rafting, rappelling, etc.) or with a team-building exercise (indoor or outdoor). This tends to create a relaxed and meaningful relational context for effective relationship development. These are good ways to begin a one-on-one mentoring relationship as well as to "break the ice" and move into more meaningful conversations and issues.

Elements of Friendship

Although each of us will meet hundreds, possibly thousands, of people in our lifetimes, only a handful of those meetings will result in relationships that remain significant for extended periods of time, and only one or two for an entire lifetime. What kind of human traits draw us into friendship? What qualities do we look for in others? For many men, developing a deeper, meaningful friendship like a mentoring relationship will require the development of some new skills and the time to develop them. In *Men Without Friends*, David W. Smith provides a list of "basic human traits [that] draw men together. Each of the six requires an element of love. They overlap somewhat, but they are useful to consider separately [when discussing] friendship qualities."[3]

1. *Acceptance*. Carl Rogers, noted psychologist, remarks that if we learn to accept others, we must "destroy the idea of what a person should be."

2. *Empathy*. More than just talk, empathy and understanding means entering into people's lives. (Some of the deepest friendships develop during sorrow.)

3. *Listening*. As a major ingredient in friendship building, genuine listening is an act of recognition. In a sense it says, "You are important to me. I care about you and what you say."

4. *Loyalty*. Quality friendships endure the test of time mainly because of the loyalty of friends.

5. *Self-disclosure*. To open up is to take a risk, to become vulnerable, to show your true side. But if you don't, you may be viewed as unapproachable and controlling, and friendships will remain superficial.

6. *Compromise*. Friends compromise on matters of personal convenience, not on matters of personal values or principles.[4]

These elements of friendship characterize a healthy mentoring relationship. But we are not seeking merely a friendship. We are seeking *intimate* relationships.

Men and Intimacy

Intimacy is not a word that many North American men use regularly in their vocabularies, nor is it something they often experience. Yet intimacy is something that most find very satisfying when they do experience it. Intimacy exists in a relationship characterized by closeness, understanding and confidentiality. It is being yourself and being understood for who you really are. Lived out in the context of a mutual relationship, it is also empowering, providing the confidence and strength to move ahead in significance and effectiveness. Intimacy is a highly desired commodity in any relationship—with God, a good friend or even a mentor.

Since one of the goals of mentoring is to develop a balanced life, establishing healthy relationships are foundational to the development of a protégé. According to Gordon MacDonald, people (men in particular) need intimate relationships on at least four levels, all of which foster the creation of a balanced life.[5] The first level of intimacy is with friends of the same gender. Men need other men, and women need other women. Men need times to simply be *men*, to talk about and do "man stuff," to be understood as a man grappling with faith, parenting, being a husband, aging, work, loneliness, feelings or fears of failure and what it means to be a man. The peer mentoring relationship can be used as a vehicle for this kind of talk. (This model will be discussed at greater length in chapter 12.) This model is particularly useful for helping men who are in the same stage of life to talk through the issues they are facing and the ways they are coping or not coping.

The second level of intimacy is in a relationship with a mentor or trusted, older friend. There are things in life that can only be seen clearly through the eyes of experience and wisdom. I lost my father to a heart attack when I was fifteen, but I was able to count on several trusted, older male friends during the early years of my adulthood and ministry. These were men who listened to me, shared some wisdom with me, included my wife and me in outings, gave me insight into life, marriage, sexuality, parenting, finance, Scripture, ministry and much more. Conversations that include the deeper issues of life, maturity and sexuality are deeply needed to help both younger and older leaders in development.

The third level of intimacy involves one's spouse (if married), and the ability to be yourself, to be understood and accepted for who you are. This intimacy includes emotional, intellectual, spiritual and sexual closeness; it is an intercourse of life as a whole. Surveys reveal that many women desire stronger spiritual leadership from their husbands; they want their husbands to pray with them regularly and study the Scriptures with them. *They desire spiritual intimacy with their spouses.* Other studies reveal that wives often complain that their husbands do not listen to them. *They desire emotional intimacy with their spouses.* Many Christian couples agree that there is not enough romance and/or sex in their marriages. *They desire sexual intimacy with their spouses.* All of these are intimacy issues that require a commitment of time, understanding and priority. Including questions and conversations about the marriage relationship in the mentoring context is often both needed and welcomed.

The fourth level of intimacy involves God. This is the relationship upon which all others must be built, according to MacDonald. The best of human relationships pales in the presence of a closeness with God. He offers the intimacy, closeness, understanding, strength and comfort we crave, but He also brings caution, conviction, rebuke and direction as correctives. In a healthy relationship with God we find the key elements to healthy human and mentoring relationships. Yet because many people (men in particular) don't know how to have this level of relationship with others (regardless of gender), it is also difficult, if not impossible, for them to connect with God at this level.

> The mentoring relationship can be a context for the development of each level of intimacy in our lives.

As we have discussed, relationships on all four levels are lacking in many men's lives. However, as healthy relationships are modeled and experienced through the mentoring relationship and intimacy with God, and then trickled down to other human relationships, young leaders can be empowered on all levels. Intimacy with same-gendered friends, older friends, spouses and God serve as a foundation for personal, professional and spiritual development. The mentoring relationship can be a context for the development of each of these levels of intimacy in our lives.

Men and Accountability

Accountability, like discipline, is one of those things that everyone knows they need, but very few really crave or seek it. Besides that, few people seem to even know how to do it effectively. For some, accountability carries with it a negative overtone of answering for areas one has neglected, failed in or otherwise not measured up in. But accountability is best set in a context of nurturing rather than simply recounting one's failures to a culturally set standard of ideals.

I have participated in and know of several men's small groups that have been able to capture a healthy blend of nurture and accountability. The protocol is as follows: Each participant gives an account of what he wants to be in his life, faith, marriage, family, ministry and dreams. He paints a picture with broad, sweeping strokes of the kind of man of God he really desires to be and the possible hindrances to realizing that goal. Each member of the group then takes on the ministry of praying for, encouraging and nurturing that person in order to reach the expressed goal. It is common for members to receive phone calls, notes through the mail or a fax or e-mail expressing a particular verse or prayer that is offered for them that day.

At the next meeting, each man shares how his goal was realized that week and, if necessary, ways in which he fell short. The goal-oriented approach, the nurturing environment and the strong encouragement are a welcome addition to a busy week and also a means of capturing the essence of effective accountability. This structure is useful as a peer-mentoring model and can also be adapted to the one-on-one mentoring relationship. (For more information on types of mentoring, see chapters 4 and 12.)

A helpful tool in establishing a goal-oriented approach is the use of an "outcome frame." The questions that form the frame are:

1. What is the goal or desired state? What do you want?

2. When and where and with whom do you want it?
3. How will you know when you get it?
4. In what ways will your life be different when you get it?
5. What stops you from getting it? What do you need in order to get it?

These questions aid the mentoring process in several ways. First, they keep the focus on the future, establishing a clear direction in which to head. Second, they serve as a developmental reorientation tool to keep from falling into a continuous problem-solving mode. Finally, they serve as an objective guideline by which to measure growth and development.

In grappling with the issues of accountability, Patrick Morley uses the "accountability iceberg" to distinguish between the "visible" you and the "real" you.

THE ACCOUNTABILITY ICEBERG[6]

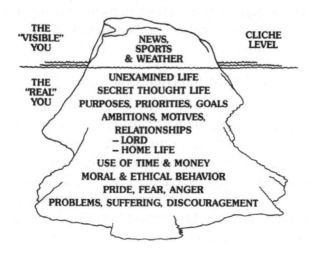

This figure clearly shows what men typically reveal to the world and what they hide. A mentoring relationship should explore all of the hidden issues.

In *The Man in the Mirror*, Morley notes the key areas in which all of us need accountability:

1. Relationship with God
2. Relationship with [spouse]
3. Relationship with kids
4. Use of time and money
5. Moral and ethical behavior
6. Areas of personal struggle[7]

Gordon MacDonald, in *Rebuilding Your Broken World*, lists twenty-six questions that each person in a mentoring relationship needs to be asked and be accountable for regularly. These questions can be found in Appendix 2 of this book.

In mentoring relationships, openly examining the previously unexamined aspects of one's private life is one of the biggest and scariest steps in developing toward personal wholeness and being conformed to the image of Christ.

The Impact of a Trusted Friendship

The development of trusted friendships that grow, develop and change as participants mature and bring their unique experiences into the relationship are at the beginning and very heart of mentoring. What a joy it has been for me to observe the growth process in myself, in other members of groups and in mentorees, and to see the reality of Christ emerge over the years! One man's story sticks in my mind:

Everyone thought Todd was quite a guy, but often no one knew how to define him beyond that statement. He was involved in an intentional mentoring group along with twenty-five other young leaders. He was a tall, strongly built, articulate, nearly overpowering African-American pastor in his thirties. As Todd came into the group he was unsure of how he fit in, and others were unsure how to interact with him. At first he wasn't sure if he even belonged. Through the two years that the group met, Todd went through various stages of acceptance and a plethora of other feelings from alienation to inclusion to frustration to adaptation. The group challenged him, and he was a challenge to the group. Near the end of the two years, Todd went through some deep, personal experiences in his life—experiences of loss, abandonment and rejection. The only two things he could count on were the stability of his marriage and the security of his relationship with God.

It was through the most difficult times that Todd began to understand the power of the relationships he had with the other men in the group, a power that he had never experienced before. Not only did the men care for and stand with him during those dark moments, but some traveled hundreds of miles, changed their schedules and went out of their way to be with him. One influential leader within the group began a personal mentoring relationship with Todd. He said to Todd, "Tell me what you want this relationship to be like, and I will do everything I can to make sure it happens." Todd took that pledge seriously. He even challenged it, taking it to its fullest extent and almost questioning its sincerity.

At every turn, that leader and the group responded positively to Todd. He has gotten through the most difficult times of his life now, and the impact of these men on his life has been profound. It has taken him to new levels of understanding God. It has given him a greater vision of the Church. It has brought new levels of intimacy to his relationships. It has made him a far more effective minister.

Todd's story can be multiplied a thousand times if we can only capture the power of effective friendships and relationships in the kingdom of God. The growth, learning and trust that Todd experienced can be available to anyone who participates in a safe, intimate mentoring relationship. We need only to create these contexts in our lives for ourselves and for others.

Key Thoughts from This Chapter

1. A healthy mentoring relationship involves asking key questions and then listening for reflections more than it is about the mentor talking, lecturing or even preaching.
2. David Smith outlines six "friendship qualities":
   a. Acceptance
   b. Empathy
   c. Listening
   d. Loyalty
   e. Self-disclosure
   f. Compromise
3. Men want and need intimacy at four key levels, according to Gordon MacDonald:
   a. Same-sex friends
   b. Mentor
   c. Spouse

    d. God

4. To reach your desired goals, utilize the five key questions of the "outcome frame":

    a. What is the goal or desired state? What do you want?

    b. When and where and with whom do you want it?

    c. How will you know when you get it?

    d. In what ways will your life be different when you get it?

    e. What stops you from getting it? What do you need in order to get it?

Questions for Further Reflection

1. Make a list of a few good friendships you have experienced in your life. Identify two or three key characteristics of those relationships. Are you still connected to those people? If not, why not? Could you go back to reconnect with them at this time?

2. Describe your most significant friendship with someone of the same gender. How often do you connect with that person? Who initiates the contact?

3. When you think of the possibility of more meaningful friendships, what do you hope to receive in those relationships and what do you see yourself contributing to the friendships?

Action Plan

1. Begin to identify your own desire for more meaningful friendships. Make an initial list of

names of people with whom you could potentially have closer relationships.
2. Make a list of items you are able to contribute to a meaningful friendship.
3. Initiate the process of seeking new friendships.

Notes

1. Stuart Miller, *Men and Friendship* (Los Angeles: Jeremy P. Tarcher, 1983), p. xiii.
2. David W. Smith, *The Friendless American Male* (Ventura, CA: Regal Books, 1983), pp. 53-63.
3. David W. Smith, *Men Without Friends: A Guide to Developing Lasting Relationships* (Nashville: Thomas Nelson, 1990), p. 87.
4. Ibid.
5. Gordon MacDonald, *The Tests Men Face* (Brantford, Ontario: Women Alive, n.d.) (audio recording).
6. Patrick Morley, *The Man in the Mirror: Solving the 24 Problems Men Face* (Grand Rapids: Zondervan, 2000), p. 277.
7. Ibid.

4

Unique Mentoring Models

AT THE AGE OF thirty-two a good friend of mine was a college administrator demonstrating high levels of competence and the ability to make quick decisions, see all sides of a situation and make the right call. John was born at the tail end of the baby boom, and he seemed to be able to understand the value and uniqueness of the generational differences between older administrators and Generation-X students. The president of the college where John worked, along with a couple of other college presidents, began to have conversations with John about his future as a top-level college administrator. They told him how he could be a president by age forty. But every conversation included some changes that John would have to make, values he would have to adjust or patterns he would have to develop.

From John's perspective, the administrators were each trying to mold him to become like them, as if each one was the ideal model of a college president. John was frustrated that his unique package of gifts and strengths, which had already emerged, was overlooked as his colleagues coached him on how to develop his strengths and character in order to adopt their personal styles.

John's experience is not uncommon. In many organizations, young leaders are either squeezed into one-size-fits-all molds or encouraged to become replicas of whoever is mentoring them. This seems to ring true across the board.

To allow one model of mentoring to be *the* model for developing leaders is similar to assuming that one size of clothing will fit every person and make each person look his or her absolute best. By divine design, each person is a distinct, unique individual with idiosyncrasies, quirks and strengths that express individuality and in many ways dictate effectiveness. Therefore, mentoring models need to be adapted in order to suit individual needs—and more than one model can work for one mentoring relationship.

> By divine design, each person is a distinct, unique individual. Therefore, mentoring models need to be adapted in order to suit individual needs.

As we look through the Bible, a number of different models and patterns emerge that reflect how different people develop with uniquely different expectations and patterns. This chapter will address five patterns of mentoring models from Scripture: the One-to-One Model, the One-to-Two Model, the Group Mentoring Model, the Unique Individual Model and the Timid and Reluctant Leader Model.

The One-to-One Model: Elijah and Elisha

The account of Elijah and his relationship with Elisha is an example of the "classic" mentoring model (see 2

Kings 2). Here, an established veteran takes an emerging leader under his or her care to model, teach and demonstrate a particular craft. The young leader acts as a shadow, watches the master at work, sees the highs and lows of the master's work and dreams his or her own dream of what ministry will be. The biblical account of Elijah and Elisha's relationship demonstrates how they went through life and ministry together and how the mentoree learned about life, faith, truth and skill from the mentor. As the torch was passed, Elisha had seen enough of what it took and was inspired by the desire to be effective in his own ministry so he asked for a "double portion" of his master's spirit (2 Kings 2:9). A double portion—because he had been moved by the mentoring spirit and personally wanted to make a significant impact of his own.

Even today, when emerging leaders see the ways in which God has blessed and used the life of a mentor, many still ask God for the blessing of the "double portion." Once they have seen effective ministry modeled for them and they see the fantasy of effective ministry move to the reality of effective ministry, they desire to emulate that effectiveness.

The One-to-Two Model: Moses, Joshua and Caleb

It was clear from the beginning whom God had appointed to lead His people out of Egypt and into the Promised Land. There was no doubt that Moses was God's chosen and anointed leader. But at one point in the forty years of Israel's wandering in the desert, it also became clear that Moses would not be the one who actually led the children of Israel into the Promised Land (see Numbers 20:12). A transition in leadership would be required in order to complete the mission.

From the earliest days of Israel's story, two young warrior-type leaders are mentioned consistently (see Numbers 14, 26; Joshua 14, 15). From spying out the land to casting a tactical vision to descriptions of their character, Joshua and Caleb are not only mentioned together but were both with Moses at strategic moments in the unfolding story of God's work with the children of Israel. Ultimately, Joshua was God's choice to replace Moses. From a human perspective, I would have chosen Caleb for his passion and his different spirit, but God's choice was Joshua. The criteria were not credentials or successes but simply the choice of God.

Many organizations try to either develop or find a successor to the current leader. In other instances, as an organization or ministry grows and needs more than one leader, a search will go forth to find the right person for the job. And yet many times it is a challenge to find that "right" person. Although it is more costly and time-consuming in the beginning, it seems to play out better in the long run to mentor a team or group of people, each of whom may well become the future leader or part of the next generation of leaders for the organization, institution or ministry. There are often too many variables and factors in a developmental mentoring equation to simply select the right person to be developed. And yet out of a pool of prospects God will often make it clear which is His candidate, even when more objective or organizational factors would not necessarily indicate the same choice.

From the scriptural model of Moses, Joshua and Caleb, we can clearly see that in our human power we cannot choose one ideal person for leadership. Rather, both people are mentored and developed together. Eventually they go in different directions or take on different roles within the same organization. Although Joshua was chosen to lead the people of Israel into the Promised Land and fulfill the mission and vision God had given to Moses, Caleb at age eighty-five also remained true to his vision, character, faith and role in the community (see Joshua 14:6-14). The goal of this kind of mentoring is to develop vision and courage, character and humility in *both* leaders. Regardless of which roles the emerging leaders take, their personal qualities and leadership character will be nearly identical.

The Group Mentoring Model: The Twelve Disciples

The third model found in Scripture is the group or team concept. Jesus' development of the twelve disciples serves as a model of group mentoring. His work with them was technically discipling because it consisted primarily of spiritual development. But, He also worked with them in areas of mentoring and intentional leadership development. He gave them principles of leadership, taught skill acquisition, demonstrated spiritual authority and power and gave them evaluative and corrective frameworks for determining the effectiveness of their mission.

In working with a large, intentional mentoring group, there are some unpredictable patterns that play their way through the process simply because of the large number of participants. Will everyone at least get along? What internal and external relational factors will come into play? How will individuals deal with their own successes and failures and those of their peers? What character issues or flaws will emerge in the process and will they be addressed thoroughly and openly? It is crucial not only to build relationships between the mentor and each individual of the group, but also between the individuals within the group.

As with Jesus' disciples, some tensions may arise between group members that will have to be addressed. Natural pairs or groupings will also emerge and become the core (like James, Peter and John), and sometimes even one special relationship with an individual (such as the relationship between Jesus and John, "the disciple whom Jesus loved" [John 13:23]) will emerge. Although these types of pairings or special groupings can cause some mild concerns for group dynamics, it needs to be noted that within all healthy group relationships there will be some individuals who are naturally drawn to each other. There will also be individuals you may like, respect, work well with and even admire, but with whom you do not bond to as well in a more intimate setting (i.e., become "friends" with outside of the group). Understanding this is part of group development and individual maturity and will help maintain a healthy, functional group.

Who and what will be the major contributors to group dynamics, direction and outcomes? On one hand, it is encouraging to see the ways God uses some people beyond what had initially seemed possible. On the other, some do not respond as well and seem to place limitations on their own effectiveness. When Jesus began with the twelve disciples, it was hard to predict who would rise to the top, who would develop quickly, who might lag behind and who would betray

Him. Who would have picked Simon Peter, with the greatest number of setbacks and the most significant failures, as the first who would pick up the bat after Jesus' death? Who would have expected him to step up to the plate on the Day of Pentecost and hit a home run with his empowered sermons (see Acts 2)? It is nearly impossible to pick which members will emerge at the end as those who exude Christlikeness and character and will continue to live out what was developed while they were with the group. It is more important in the group mentoring setting to facilitate growth and learning for all participants and to give them all room to err, succeed and hit a home run.

I have been a part of several mentoring groups (for new converts, for college students, for seminary interns and in intentional leadership development) as well as the leader of several groups. I have seen many of the principles and patterns of Jesus' development of the twelve disciples play out in the lives of emerging leaders from these groups even to this day. There are many reasons to mentor in a group and others that make group mentoring difficult. Particularly, the challenges that group dynamics present can often dissuade a mentor from beginning a group or can squash a group's development when it is already up and running. However, these groups can also foster learning from the other participants. They take pressure off the leader to be the "guru." They facilitate mentoring a number of people in a shorter period of time. And the ultimate benefit of this mentoring framework is that it teaches the members of the group to interact with each other on a personal basis—a situation with which women are generally comfortable but that most men have not experienced.

The group becomes a terrific learning ground for men to experience friendships, trust and intimacy as well as leadership development and Christlike character.

The Unique Individual Model: Jesus and Peter

This model and the one that follows it are actually one-to-one models. However, both of them are distinctive because of the unique character of the individual who is being mentored. Quite often in a group of 25 young leaders who were selected out of a pool of 200-300, 2 or 3 of them are noticeably more distinct and unique even among their highly gifted peers. This and the following model work with examples of such kinds of leaders.

As a mentor, our Lord Jesus Christ rose to a level that none have matched since. He took a dozen men and developed them to carry out a dramatic and divine mission. As Robert Clinton states:

> Jesus saw in these simple men the potential of leadership. They were indeed unlearned and ignorant from the world's standard but were teachable. Though often mistaken in their judgments and slow to comprehend spiritual things, they were harvest men, willing to confess their need. Their mannerisms may have been awkward and their abilities limited. . . . What is perhaps most significant about them is their sincere yearning for God and the realities of His life.[1]

The disciples were unique from one another, and in some ways they were unique from their peers. Most unique among the group, however, was Simon Peter. Jesus' mentoring relationship with Peter is a classic example of mentoring an individual with unique needs and talents. Peter's profile is intriguing: He was passionate, compulsive, likeable and prone to making mistakes. Although his heart was right, often his responses were not. Peter always had a response to situations—whether it was getting out of the boat to walk on the water or pulling out a sword in order and cutting off the ear of the soldier who came to arrest Jesus at Gethsemane—although he rarely seemed to understand the implications of his actions.

There are many patterns of mentoring that will fit limitless situations and individuals. The individuals are out there. They want and need to be mentored.

And yet, in spite of all this, Jesus chose Peter not only as one of the twelve disciples but as one of the inner circle of three who were with Him at special moments in His life: at the Mount of Transfiguration (see Matthew 17:1-13) and at Gethsemane on His last night on earth (see 26:36-46). Why was this commitment and devotion given to someone like Peter? In part because Jesus saw what Peter was becoming—what the developed Peter could become.

And Jesus was right! From the sermon on the Day of Pentecost that brought more than 3,000 converts to faith in Jesus (see Acts 2:41) to the setting of the New Testament policy (see Acts 15) to the writing of two significant New Testament epistles, Simon Peter's influence was dramatic.

Do you know any Simon Peters? They lack some polish. They speak out of turn. They give the answer without adequately understanding the question. They may need some additional Ritalin. But underneath it all is a passionate heart for God and some unique and powerful gifting just waiting to be developed.

The Timid and Reluctant Leader Model: Paul and Timothy

In the mentoring process certain mentorees will stand out for various reasons—some for their abilities, some because they are go-getters, some because of character, charm or a key quality and some because they seem to "have what it takes" but are for some reason reluctant or timid. Although it may take a bit longer to identify the reluctant or timid individual's merits or develop an appreciation for his or her abilities, after a time it becomes clear that the key elements of leadership are present; the individual is just hesitant for some reason. Don't pass on the opportunity to mentor someone such as this!

The Apostle Paul had a young leader he sought to mentor named Timothy, who was one of these timid leaders. Paul wrote the following to him in Second Timothy 1:3-8:

> I thank God, whom I serve, as my forefathers did, with a clear conscience, as night and day I constantly remember you in my prayers. Recalling your tears, I long to see you, so that I may be filled with joy. I have been reminded of your sincere faith, which first lived in your grandmother Lois and in your mother Eunice and, I am persuaded, now lives in you also. For this reason I remind you to fan into flame the gift of God, which is in you through the laying on of my hands. For God did not give us a spirit of timidity, but a spirit of power, of love and of self-discipline.
>
> So do not be ashamed to testify about our Lord, or ashamed of me his prisoner. But join with me in suffering for the gospel, by the power of God.

In this letter Paul is assuring Timothy of the key elements of his life and development, even his heritage. Paul challenges Timothy not to give in to his timidity but to take on God's power and develop life disciplines to move through his current situation.

How many significant leaders began (and even continued throughout the course of their lives) as individuals who for some reason lacked confidence, who were cautious, shy, reluctant, timid or reserved or who appeared inwardly or outwardly to be progressing slowly in their development? History has shown that it is not necessarily the runner who is fastest out of the blocks who wins the race. It is often a common pattern that those who take longer to come into their own as leaders finish well and strongly. Consider spending some extra time with a timid or reluctant emerging leader to find out if he or she has what it takes but is just off to a slow start. It could pay off in the long run.

A Model for Every Mentoree

We have looked at five unique patterns of mentoring from Scripture. Each has its own challenges and strengths, but each also deserves careful consideration. How many Elishas are out there who could benefit from intentional modeling and mentoring from a proven leader? How many emerging leaders could make a great contribution to the team as mentorees, working together through various developmental stages and accomplishing significant amounts, all while serving the Creator's cause? And imagine the potential of a group of six, ten or twelve carefully selected emerging leaders who have effective ministry modeled, taught and evaluated for them? Imagine the future impact of their lives even after you are gone!

How many characters out there are like Simon Peter—highly motivated, passionate, impulsive, prone to making mistakes, but with a great heart? Imagine intentionally mentoring them through to maturity. Imagine the benefits for the cause of Christ! How many timid Timothys are there who have the background but need to know how to appropriate the authority and power of Jesus Christ?

There are many patterns of mentoring that will fit limitless situations and individuals. The individuals are out there; they are all over; you know them. They want and need to be mentored and developed as leaders.

Key Thoughts from This Chapter

1. Observe various models and patterns of mentoring in Scripture:
   a. The One-to-One Model: Elijah and Elisha
   b. The One-to-Two Model: Moses, Joshua and Caleb
   c. The Group Mentoring Model: The Twelve Disciples
   d. The Unique Individual Model: Jesus and Peter
   e. The Timid and Reluctant Leader Model: Paul and Timothy
2. Tailor mentoring models to fit each person's uniqueness and stage of development.

Questions for Further Reflection

1. What are your thoughts on the five mentoring models listed in this chapter? Which model(s)

might best fit where you are in your current process of development? Why did you make that choice?

2. Is there someone you know who could benefit from one of the unique models but may have never seen him- or herself that way? Discuss it with that person.

Action Plan

1. In order to be mentored most effectively, begin to determine your unique needs and stage of development.
2. In order to mentor more effectively, begin to explore which of the models best fits the potential mentorees in your life.

Note

1. J. Robert Clinton, *The Making of a Leader: Recognizing the Lessons and Stages of Leadership Development* (Colorado Springs: NavPress, 1988), p. 197.

5

The Developmental Process

THE DEMAND FOR LEADERSHIP is ever-present, especially within the Church. What sort of process builds character and integrity, heart and soul, vision and confidence, skill and ability to lead?

A primary focus of mentoring is to aid and guide emerging leaders through the key developmental stages of their lives. Some emerging leaders will go through these stages naturally, and even in order. For others, the mentoring process will require more coaching, because they may have missed or not fully developed through a stage. A stronger focus on coaching and mentoring will enable healthy and complete development.

The developmental processes of life are as simple as seeing life in a series of stages, much like the alphabet. Without compartmentalizing life too much, it is natural for individuals to move from stages A through D as they are on their way to R, ultimately to reach Z. If life can be seen as a natural progression with developmental stages, then these stages can be viewed as healthy developments of one's life. If we think of life in this way, then the developmental process becomes a natural way to view life and its successes and failures.

The emergence of a leader, especially a pastoral leader, must also be viewed as a developmental process with stages and life experiences in each area. Although major differences in individual paths will occur, there will be great similarities in the overall process for each individual. And, this process and these experiences are much more productive in the life of the developing leader when there is the wisdom and experience of a mentor to help with reflection and to aid in direction.

Elijah's Developmental Process

In First Kings 18, the story of the prophet Elijah offers a significant case study of how the developmental process works in the realm of faith. Preachers have painted amazing pictures of Elijah on Mount Carmel, standing seemingly alone before God and the people of Israel against the 450 prophets of Baal and Asherah. He stood with a prophetic gaze in his eye and the power of God in his soul against the great forces of darkness, calling down fire from heaven and winning one of the greatest battles in history for Almighty God. The story behind the story, however, starts a chapter earlier.

God walked the emerging prophet through the stages of development so that when he stood on Mount Carmel it was a natural step for him—and one he'd never thought of before. In First Kings 17, we see Elijah in the first stage of his faith development. In verses 1-6, God makes it clear to Elijah that he is to go down by the river where the ravens will take care of him, and he should drink from the brook and rest. God asks Elijah to go away and simply trust Him for his daily needs. He is to *put all of his trust upon God*. This is a necessary step for us a Christians if we're truly going to be used by God beyond our own ability. The first principle of developing faith, then, is *trust*.

The second step of Elijah's process comes in verses 7-16, where God sends him to the widow of Zarephath. He goes to the widow and asks if she will feed him. She is down on her luck and proclaims that she has next to nothing left. Her plan was to take the food that she has, feed herself and her son and then die. Elijah assures her that he has been sent by God and that her job is to take what she has and feed him. This passage tells us that in the development of our faith there comes a time when our trust in God goes past just trusting for ourselves: It involves *bringing other people into our sphere of faith.* Trusting God isn't just a personal thing that happens alone with Him. Its impact influences the lives of other people as well.

As Elijah journeys to Mount Carmel, the third developmental stage comes in verses 17 to the end of the chapter, where the widow's son dies. Elijah returns to the widow, goes into a room alone with the boy and, in an act of faith, stretches himself over the boy three times and asks God for the truly miraculous. And God, in His sovereignty, responds and brings the widow's son back to life. For Elijah to successfully go to Mount Carmel and face the opposition there, he had to be able to *trust God for the truly miraculous.* But please note, he did it without an audience. No one else was there. It was Elijah, the dead boy and God.

The confidence that came to him, the strengthening of his faith and the developmental processes that took place here were foundational for him to move toward Mount Carmel in chapter 18. Now, with the prophet

Elijah boldly standing on Mount Carmel representing God, the faith of all of Israel is on the line and the truly miraculous is required for the people of God to move on in a healthy relationship with Him. So there stands the man, the prophet, the chosen servant of God, Elijah. This was not the first time his faith had to be strong. We can see the stages God had walked him through in preparation for the "big event." The principle of this passage is the fourth developmental stage: Elijah *trusted God for the miraculous in front of a multitude of people* with a great deal at stake (including the future history of the people of God).

> A primary focus of mentoring is to aid and guide emerging leaders through the key developmental stages of their lives.

Although there was more at stake in the life of Elijah than is true for the average person, both the stages and the outcomes are similar. As we are conformed to the image of Christ, as the fullness of God is formed within us, it is necessary for us to move from one developmental stage to the next. It doesn't just happen. It isn't something that we can do by ourselves. It is a process in which God is uniquely involved, whereby experiences and circumstances play a key role. It is all a part of God's overall plan of working with us.

The Developmental Process

The developmental process includes stages of development, the nature of change and desired outcomes. In *The-*

ories of Developmental Psychology, Patricia Miller provides a useful resource that allows a closer look into developmental theories. Although most of her applications focus on children, much of her rhetoric offers useful guidelines for human development in general. Miller states that developmental change has four critical issues:

1. What is the basic nature of humans?
2. Is development qualitative or quantitative?
3. How do nature and nurture contribute to development?
4. What is it that develops?[1]

As for her first question, "What is the basic nature of humans?" we know that the work of God is to transform the darker side of the human soul and to transform the individual from the inside out (see Romans 6). God desires to restore His image and that of His Son in a lifelong developmental transformation (see Romans 8:29).

As for Miller's second question, "Is development qualitative or quantitative?" God's desire is to bring about qualitative change within the individual life and in a person's character. The work of transformational development is by nature qualitative.

Biblical patterns give evidence to both tenets of her third question, "How do nature and nurture contribute to development?" Moses and Joshua were uniquely different in nature. In reference to Moses, the text states, "No prophet has risen in Israel like Moses" (Deuteronomy 34:10). By nature Moses was uniquely gifted. It was Joshua, however, who was able to finish the mission after Moses died—a significant feat indeed. In addition to nature, their unique experiences set each apart so that their lives unfolded in uniquely different ways.

Finally, to answer Miller's fourth question, "What is it that develops?" what actually develops in the life of the individual Christian are Christlike character traits. The pattern of Romans 5:3-4 is a qualitative summary: Trials produce perseverance; perseverance produces character; character produces hope, both temporal and eternal.

In his book *The Making of a Leader*, Bobby Clinton describes five phases of lifelong development.[2] These phases include all of life's processes and experiences.

PHASE 1: Sovereign foundation
PHASE 2: Inner growth
PHASE 3: Life maturity
PHASE 4: Ministry maturity
PHASE 5: Convergence

In phase one, the building blocks of life emerge. Personality characteristics emerge and character traits are embedded. In phase two, emerging leaders typically receive some training, both formal and informal. Even though the focus of the training may be an academic program or a ministry experience, a major thrust of God's development of the individual is primarily inward. The real training is in the heart of a person whom God intentionally develops. In phase three, the emerging leader enters into ministry as the primary focus of his or her life. Although the training may be informal (projects, workshops, etc.), the major activities are conducted in ministry. The unique aspect of phases one, two and three is God's primary work in, not through, the emerging leader. In phase four, mature fruitfulness comes as the leader identifies and uses his or her "gift-mix" with power. Clinton states that, although the developmental process appears to be sequential, in real life, phases three and four often overlap. In phase five, role, gift-mix, experience, temperament, etc., all come together. Sadly, according to Clinton, not many leaders experience this convergence. Promotions and positions often limit them from using their unique gift-mixes. But God prepares the individual for real convergence. He conforms him or her to the image of Christ (see Romans 8:28-29) and matures the leader for effectiveness in His kingdom. God's approach is to work in and then through the individual.[3]

Blocks, Barriers and Deprivations

It is significant to note that in the developmental process there can be *blocks* in our development, placed there by our own unwillingness, by other people or by circumstances of life. To the individual, blocks look like limitations, hills or mountains to climb, fears or panic, and they can even result in emotional and developmental paralysis. Blocks prevent us from moving forward in our development.

In dealing with blocks, it can be helpful to observe personal "self talk" patterns for phrases like "I can't do this," "It's too big or too bad," "It's hopeless. I'll never be able to do it," "I've tried but it won't go away," "No matter what, I fail at it every time" or "It will never be good enough." If phrases like this show up in self-talk, they should be addressed as potential blocks with a mentor, friend or counselor.

In addition to blocks, there can also be *barriers* that do not stop, but rather slow down a person's development. Like blocks, barriers can be seen as limitations, but they are less permanent and smaller than blocks. They tend to make the issues we are facing appear to be more challenging than they really are, but unlike blocks, barriers are often things that can be gone around or over. They are temporary or simply require additional processing through counseling, prayer or talking.

A third deterrent in the developmental process is *deprivations* that explicitly hinder a person's development. Deprivations form when events arise in a person's life that significantly hinder the individual from fully developing in one particular stage. As we look at our lives, we can find deprivations by looking back on the stages of our development and seeing where we've missed something. Perhaps we have missed the development of a foundation of security, love, self-esteem, affirmation, intimacy or significance in our lives.

I grew up in a happy, rural, midwestern home. I was the youngest of four children in a family that offered significant amounts of security, love and laughter. It was a great place to be while I was growing up—until I was ten years old. At that time, my grandfather, who lived on the farm next to us and with whom we worked and farmed, died suddenly. A few months later, my oldest brother was in a serious car accident, lived six weeks in a coma and died of massive head injuries. His loss changed our family in a significant way. For me it was not only the loss of fun and laughter in our house; it changed the makeup of my entire family. Only a few years later, another brother was drafted into the marines and sent to Vietnam in the thick of the war. While he was in Vietnam, my sister went to college 1,000 miles away, so I was home alone with my mother and father. That same year, my father, who was forty-nine, had a massive heart attack and died suddenly. The big, happy family with lots of laughter and security had changed dramatically. I was only fifteen.

At that stage in my development, I needed many things. Most of them were not available because of the events that had occurred in my life. A number of developmental gaps resulted that would later surface. When I was a thirty-year-old pastor in the midst of a good ministry and graduate studies, married with four young children, my wife revealed to me that she was having difficulty in our marriage. She said to me, "I feel like I'm married to a thirty-year-old man who is really a sixteen-year-old boy emotionally. Would you please figure out how to develop emotionally, the way you have physically, spiritually, intellectually and academically?" She was on to something and I began my journey.

> The developmental process is far more than skill acquisition. It is about issues of heart, character and integrity and personal, emotional and spiritual development.

Through mentoring, practicing spiritual disciplines such as journaling and fasting and participating in classic counseling, I was able to understand the developmental deprivations that had surfaced in my life. I thank my wife Dianna for her patience, God for His faithfulness and presence and those significant people who took the time to build into my life the developmental stages I had missed.

Mentoring Does Make a Difference

Understanding the developmental process is crucial to the mentoring relationship. It is far more than skill acquisition. It is about issues of heart, character and integrity and personal, emotional and spiritual development. It is about moving as a congruent, whole person from point A to D on the way to R and on to the goal of finishing up at Z.

As the next generation of leaders emerges from Generations X and Y, much is being written about how uniquely different they are as a group and as individuals from the Builder and Boomer Generations. If Generations X and Y are going to develop well as leaders, and if the Church is going to move strongly into the twenty-first century, it is the responsibility of the mentors to understand the new generations. They need their mentors to understand their uniqueness as individuals, the implications of the world in which they grew up, their understanding and development of life and faith, how to aid and guide their development and how to incorporate the principles of mentoring, coaching and spiritual direction into their lives.

These new leaders need to be ready when the time comes for them to stand on the mountain, in the arena, in the university or wherever God has called them to stand. They need the heart, passion, strength and experiential base of a modern-day Elijah—to risk faith with the confidence and assurance that God is with them, to stand and make a difference for the generation after them. They need someone to walk with them through their developmental stages and explore any blocks, barriers or deprivations just as much as they need faith, physical or spiritual development.

I am asked regularly with great sincerity, "Do you think mentoring really matters? Can people actually change life patterns and character issues?" The answers to these questions are not easy, nor are they easy to demonstrate. But we can confidently and to some degree conclusively say, "Yes!" through the indwelling work of the Holy Spirit working in and through the fully devoted follower of Jesus Christ. The frameworks of the mentoring relationship provide a construct that facilitates the actual process of change in the lives of individuals.

Key Thoughts from This Chapter

1. The developmental processes of life are as simple as seeing life in a series of stages. A primary focus of mentoring is to aid and guide emerging leaders through the key developmental stages of their lives.

2. Understanding developmental processes in mentoring is about issues of heart, character and integrity and personal, emotional and spiritual development.

3. Elijah's faith development process involved:
   a. Trusting God for basic needs of life
   b. Including others in your sphere of trusting God
   c. Trusting God for the miraculous (without an audience)
   d. Trusting God and risk-taking in public arenas

4. According to Bobby Clinton, there are five phases of lifelong development:
   a. Sovereign foundation
   b. Inner growth

   c. Life maturity

   d. Ministry maturity

   e. Convergence

5. Within the developmental process there can be blocks, barriers and deprivations that must be overcome in order for us to move forward.

Questions for Further Reflection

1. As you look at your life currently, how much of where you are is simply how your life has emerged naturally and how much is by intentional design? Is it time to be more intentional in your development?

2. If you were to consider issues of the heart and emotional development, what might be the next area of growth for you? Will that growth best be achieved through a structured experience, the practice of spiritual disciplines or intentional mentoring, coaching or counseling?

3. As you consider risks in your life and trusting God, what could the next stage look like for you? What might hold you back? How do you plan to address that particular issue in your life?

Action Plan

1. Identify one or two key areas of personal, emotional or spiritual development that you would benefit from at this time.

2. Identify ways that God wants you to take a risk and trust Him for things beyond your current experience of facts.

Notes

1. Patricia H. Miller, *Theories of Developmental Psychology* (New York: W.H. Freeman, 1993), p. 17.
2. J. Robert Clinton, *The Making of a Leader: Recognizing the Lessons and Stages of Leadership Development* (Colorado Springs: NavPress, 1988), pp. 30-3.
3. Ibid.

6

Spiritual Formation: Discipleship

JUST AS AN INDIVIDUAL progresses through stages of physical and emotional maturity, cognitive formation and relational development, it is also natural to progress through stages of spiritual formation, maturity and development. At times it seems as though the North American Church has given significant attention to structural design and programming in the hope of fostering spiritual development, but it appears that little attention has been given to each person's individual spiritual formation and development. Spiritual formation must begin with quality discipleship. Let's figure out how the discipleship process figures into the mentoring relationship.

The Power and Processes of Discipleship

What are the differences between mentoring and discipleship? How different are they? Some authors have suggested that the two words be used interchangeably. Well, they can't be. Discipleship, by its design and limitations, is best focused on specific spiritual maturity and developmental issues. Mentoring, however, can be used in a much broader developmental context and describes areas of development, such as skill acquisition, that go beyond the specific realm of spirituality and spiritual development. Thus, for the purposes of this book, the concept of discipleship will be used for specific spiritual development and mentoring will be used in the larger context of lifelong development.

A clear understanding of discipleship is foundational to understanding spiritual development in the New Testament. An overview of the four Gospels reflects that:

1. Jesus began His ministry by calling disciples.
2. He spent much of His time discipling His disciples.
3. When He left the earth He said to His disciples, "Go make more disciples!"

Armed with this elementary logic, we can assume that one of Jesus' primary intentions, if not His key intention, was for the Church to make disciples. Unfortunately, although discipleship may have been a main focus in the Scriptures, one does not have to reflect too deeply on the structure and goals of today's Church to see that its primary mission does not appear to follow suit.

In order to explore the concept of discipleship it is necessary to begin with a useful definition: Discipling others is a *process*. It is *not* a program. The Church typically loves programs. We love four laws, five steps, eight stages. We like twelve weeks of curriculum to fill a quarter. But discipleship was never intended to be a programmed structure only. It is a process, and as such, people go through it in different time frames. Just because someone finishes the study guide doesn't mean that he or she completely understood the material, assimilated it into his or her life and is now suddenly ready for the next stage.

Let's look at the following diagram, which presents a definition of what discipleship is and does. Then, we will dissect its meaning phrase-by-phrase in order to examine the discipling process.

	Discipling others is the process by which
Example	*a Christian with a life worth emulating*
Commitment	*commits himself*
Time	*for an extended period of time*
Numerical Limitations	*to a few individuals*
PHASE 1:	
Evangelism	*who have been won to Christ,*
Direction	*the purpose being*
Guardianship	*to aid and guide*
PHASE 2:	
Growth	*their growth to maturity and equip them*
PHASE 3:	
Reproduction	*to reproduce themselves in a third spiritual generation.*[1]

*"Discipling others is the process by which **a Christian with a life worth emulating** . . ."*

Note that "to emulate" means "to model but to go beyond." So much about the Christian life is caught rather than taught. I have noticed numerous times how people pick up various aspects of spirituality or faith simply through observation.

Years ago, I was a guest speaker in an African-American church in Brooklyn for a Sunday service. This was a church that took praying for the speaker seriously.

Prayer time began forty-five minutes before the service. Sixteen people met to pray, and the prayers were diverse and quite long. As I observed them, I was fascinated by the phrases they used and the types of prayers they said. I have had opportunities to preach in many places and in a wide variety of contexts, and I had honestly not heard these phrases before that particular instance. I was intrigued, and I must confess that I spent more time pondering the uniquenesses of the prayers than their intents.

> Discipleship, by its design and limitations,
> is best focused on specific spiritual
> maturity and developmental issues.

After more than a dozen people had prayed, I thought to myself, *I'm willing to bet that one of the last people who prays will be one of the significant prayer leaders of this congregation.* Just as I had thought, as we came to the end of the prayer time, a godly man in his fifties with a voice like God Himself prayed and used every single phrase I had heard around the circle up to that point. I thanked God for each and every one of those phrases. I also thanked Him for this discipler who had modeled prayer for the others in his congregation. After the service I inquired about this man and was told that he was the primary discipler of many people in the congregation. His particular strength was coaching people in praying prayers that made a difference.

Modeling plays a unique role in spiritual formation and leadership development. It begins with the basics of faith, including: types and patterns of prayer, how to be a giving person, how to trust God for strength and courage beyond your own, how one processes the greatest and darkest moments of life, how to cope with tragedy, failure and loss and how to address the most challenging people in your life. Most of us learn best by having lessons modeled for us, especially if we can also talk about the lessons with someone we trust.

"Discipling others is the process by which a Christian with a life worth emulating commits himself for an extended period of time . . ."

Please note that the time frame of the discipleship process cannot be defined in terms of weeks, months or years. Some people will progress rapidly through stages of learning and quickly capture the content and the heart of what they are being taught. Others will take a year or even more. The issue is not how long it takes; it's that the lessons are *taking*.

"Discipling others is the process by which a Christian with a life worth emulating commits himself for an extended period of time to a few individuals . . ."

One-on-one discipleship has been popular in Christian circles for some time. Although this kind of discipleship is often the easiest to schedule, it is not the most effective in the long run for the individual or the congregation. Small-group discipleship is far more effective for many reasons. First, it's easier to avoid the "guru" mentality, where one person has all of the answers and doles out wisdom. In a group, there is shared responsibility for input, prayers and answers. Second, group discipleship spreads the responsibility of praying for each other, so instead of one, there are numerous people nurturing and praying for each individual. Third, it motivates new believers at the beginning stages of their ministries to go deeper into spiritual development as they see more mature believers living their faith. Finally, if a person's ministry is effectively reaching unbelieving people, there will not be enough time for him or her to disciple people one-on-one. There are too many people who need to be discipled.

"Discipling others is the process by which a Christian with a life worth emulating commits himself for an extended period of time to a few individuals who have been won to Christ . . ."

It is significant to note the process outlined here. Those going through the discipleship process must understand the *conversion* process. They must be literally *Christian* rather than *Christian-ized*. The power of the Holy Spirit must dwell within them and accomplish His work from the inside out. This is different from a person who simply mentally understands Christianity. Life-change must be taking place as the Holy Spirit empowers the individual.

"Discipling others is the process by which a Christian with a life worth emulating commits himself for an extended period of time to a few individuals who have been won to Christ, the purpose being to aid and guide their growth to maturity . . ."

The purpose of discipleship is to aid and guide the disciples' growth toward maturity. Please note two things: First, a person's spiritual maturity is very hard to definitively evaluate without being either incredibly subjective on the one hand or making up a detailed list of behaviors on the other. Second, Jesus made it very clear that His disciples were to be able and willing to reproduce themselves in additional spiritual generations. For Jesus, discipleship did not end with spiritual maturity, but the spiritually mature were to model and reproduce faith in the next generation.

*"Discipling others is the process by which a Christian with a life worth emulating commits himself for an extended period of time to a few individuals who have been won to Christ, the purpose being to aid and guide their growth to maturity **and equip them to reproduce themselves in a third spiritual generation.**"*

Most definitions of discipleship stop with maturity, as if the goal is to have a Christian who has reached some sort of depth of spiritual understanding. And yet, very few have an understanding of spiritual maturity. It is defined in a wide variety of ways depending upon one's doctrinal preferences or denominational perspectives. Definitions of discipleship were never intended to end with maturity.

Discipleship at its best progresses until each and every believer is both able and willing to reproduce him- or herself in the next spiritual generation. Jesus called His disciples to Him and spent time discipling them, teaching them, showing them and modeling for them. Then He put them in circumstances where He empowered them to do ministry themselves, and when He left Earth, He told them to go make more disciples. The discipleship process goes from conversion and life-change to spiritual maturity to reproducing in the next spiritual generation. We begin as new converts and are guided to maturity. Then, we have to complete the process by discipling others and reproducing another generation of believers.

Reproducing the Next Generation

There are three steps to developing the next generation of church leaders. Begin with a refocused mission—*reproducing*. Next, expand the vision beyond local church ministry positions and see the ministry as building the kingdom of God and the larger Body of Christ. Finally, view people developmentally; see them progressing in value, service and Christlikeness. Our mission is to produce disciples who make disciples who make disciples—to the ends of the earth!

Building Confidence

Many qualified Christians suffer unnecessarily from spiritual inferiority complexes. Others simply need some assurance and confidence that God can use them. In the last few years I have held leadership conferences and discipleship seminars in over fifty local churches. In the final sessions I asked two questions:

1. Are you a mature follower of Jesus Christ, able and willing to reproduce yourself in another spiritual generation?
2. Are you in need of development in a particular aspect of life or faith first before you can become a reproducer?

In nearly every group, approximately twenty percent indicated that they were able and willing to begin reproducing themselves in another spiritual generation. I asked the other eighty percent, "What do you need to develop or change in order to reproduce yourself in another spiritual generation?" Most said, "I need confidence!" Generally, they responded this way because they had heard about discipling but had never seen it happen. They needed to be there when someone prayed to receive Christ. They needed to hear the questions that a new Christian has and also hear how those questions are answered. They needed guidance and teaching from a prayer warrior so that their own prayer lives would grow and develop. Such guidance would allow them to feel more confident.

It will take some adjustment, but ministry in the Church can be structured to develop people in this way. Christ discipled this way. Shouldn't the Church, His Bride, also disciple by His example?

Getting Involved in the Process

Once a mature Christian possesses the confidence to become a reproducer, he or she can explore the various levels of involvement available:

- Training evangelists who lead others to Christ
- Developing disciplers who disciple new converts
- Developing staff who in turn develop others in various ministries
- Developing younger potential leaders/ministers
- Training and developing the board
- Mentoring and being mentored

The process of discipling appears to be time-consuming. And it is. But the benefits far outweigh the time invested when you consider the relationships that will reproduce severalfold beyond what any one person can do alone. It is a worthwhile investment.

One way to establish time investments is to look at it as a tithe offering. If it is seen as giving time to Christ to further His kingdom, it makes sense, and it's a tangible, profitable way to give of oneself. Four, five or six hours each week or an hour every day can be taken to *purposefully* invest in the lives of people who will then reproduce themselves in yet another spiritual generation. Just as Jesus commanded His disciples to make more disciples, we can heed His call and make more disciples as well.

A Lifelong Developmental Approach

After my first fifteen years of ministry I took several days to reflect on the dramatic life-changes I had seen people go through. I had witnessed more than a thousand people make professions of faith and hundreds of people go through the discipleship process. I reflected on dramatic life-change stories and their outcomes. It was fun to celebrate successes and stories of change. It was also a little sad to realize that sometimes the life-change didn't last for more than a decade or so.

As I reflected on these lives, I wondered what the reasons were for permanent change and what should or could have been done differently in the situations where the change didn't last. I discovered one unifying characteristic in the stories of people who had lasted through the test of time: *They stayed closely connected to a local church, ministry or group of people who cared for them, discipled them, coached them and mentored them through the various stages and changes of life.* Those who tried to make it on their own or didn't stay connected relationally often were not able to permanently incorporate the initial changes they had made in their lives. The difference was the *intentional development of the person through the stages of his or her life through discipleship and mentoring.*

When people move best through the various stages of life, it is typically in the context of being in a personal relationship (such as a mentoring relationship) or having a relationship with a local church or ministry. Within those relationships, careful attention is paid to how the individuals move throughout the various aspects of their lives. As circumstances change, as they naturally move through the stages of life, there is a relational context in which they can receive encouragement, spiritual direction, questions for personal reflection and connections to people who will be there for them as needed.

> Those who excelled the most stayed closely connected to a local church, ministry or group of people who cared for them, discipled them, coached them and mentored them.

Most people develop best when they have the kinds of relationships that remain constant for them. For the Church to effectively incorporate this into its ministry, intentionality is required in philosophy of discipleship, spiritual direction and mentoring; it will also require adjustments in how the Church spends its time and resources. I usually recommend that pastors and ministry leaders in the Church begin with at least a ten-percent tithe of their time and move to a twenty-percent commitment to spend time in intentionally developing both people and structures. In the North American Church, this is often an unusual concept. Yet most missionaries who work overseas report that *at least* twenty percent of their time is *required* in this kind of ministry. It is clear that the Church around the world is growing at a quicker rate than the Church in North America. I think there is a clear connection between the success overseas and the time spent intentionally developing people.

Discipleship and mentoring are not intended to be simply "stages" that help move a person through a particular time, season or problem. Rather, both are intended to be developmental in nature and remain significant aspects of a person's growth throughout life.

Key Thoughts from This Chapter

1. Jesus' discipleship process was as follows:
   a. He began His ministry by calling disciples
   b. He spent His time discipling His disciples
   c. He challenged His disciples to go and make more disciples
2. Create a staged development approach to discipleship that intentionally tracks people through the various stages of spiritual development from conversion to a willingness and ability to reproduce their faith in the next generation.
3. In accessing life-change stories over a ten-year period, I learned that those who excelled the most stayed closely connected to a local church, ministry or group of people who cared for them, discipled them, coached them and mentored them through the various stages and changes of life.

Questions for Further Reflection

1. Are you presently a disciple of Jesus Christ who is able and willing to reproduce yourself in the next spiritual generation? Describe ways you are living this out.
2. If you are not, what resources do you need in order to be both able and willing? Will you actively pursue those resources?
3. Describe what spiritual maturity can look like for you. How close have you come to your goal? What will be the next two steps to move you closer to spiritual maturity?
4. Are you willing to commit ten percent of your time to intentionally discipling or mentoring emerging younger leaders? Describe your plan to implement this in your life.

Action Plan

1. Honestly assess both your willingness and your ability to reproduce a dynamic faith in the next generation of believers.
2. Identify areas of strength you can contribute to an emerging leader and one or two areas for you to strengthen in your own faith.

Note

1. Allen Hadidian, *Successful Discipling* (Chicago: Moody Press, 1979), pp. 31-2.

7
Character Formation

IN MY FIRST TWO years as a professor, I dealt with several hundred young men who were preparing for ministry, and I was intrigued to see that there were at least three distinct aspects of their development:

1. A heart for God
2. Their images
3. Their identities

Each of them possessed a passion for God and a desire to be a useful servant in the bigger context of His kingdom. In most cases their desires seemed to go well beyond a quest for personal significance to a genuine passion for God and His work. Many could have been—or even had previously been—successful at other ventures in life, but each had a genuine desire to invest his life specifically in the kingdom of God.

Each of them also possessed a very clear image, a public persona that they projected. The images were varied and represented a number of unique combinations: the serious Greek student, the jock, the man of prayer, the preacher, the evangelist, the wise counselor, the gifted leader, the missionary prayer group leader, the class clown, the power lifter, the ladies' man, the humble servant, the next denominational president or bishop. The list goes on.

The images were quite distinct, and many were well-polished in their presentation. But as I spoke with the young men, I learned that the image that was presented for public viewing and the real person in the chair had little in common. The image may have been incredibly convincing to the general public, but there was a whole other side of the individual—his identity—that was very different. The identity of an individual is simply what he or she is *really* like behind the public presentation. It involves self-perception, real or perceived deprivations, fears, failures (and fear of failure), various identity issues, one's sexuality, etc.—the things that go into making a person what he or she really is.

These students and young pastors were feeling a major disparity between their public personas (what people see) and the unresolved feelings that haunted them (what they perceived themselves to be). All three aspects of the individual were real: Each had a heart for God and His service; each possessed at least some of the attributes that were being reflected in the image that was presented for public viewing; but each one also had some definite unresolved identity issues that hindered his development.

Character Is a Collection of Qualities

Often people know the right things, they say the right words, they teach and preach the Scripture faithfully, and—when people are looking—they do it well. But when no one is looking, their lives tell a different story. There are some "wannabes" in this world. Maybe you know people like this. They want to be good Christians. They want to be faithful servants. They desire Christlikeness. But when the situation requires them to say no to temptation, they'll fudge. When it comes to saying yes to those dares of faith, they'll analyze things to *death* until the opportunity is past. If they are ever going to become the servants of God that they want to be (and that God wants them to be), it will take discipline, follow-through and living out the things they say they believe. That is the difference between a wannabe and a servant of God.

Character is the collection of distinctive qualities unique to each individual. It includes things like values, personality and even temperament. It covers who you are, what you do and what you know. A good way to conceptualize character is to think of it as what you are like when no one is looking. It is something you have as a person, but it is also something that inevitably shows itself in what you do.[1]

I tell people—especially men—the following all the time: "A good way to gauge this character thing is when you are away from home, traveling. It's midnight. You are in a city where no one knows you. What do you do? Where do your thoughts go? Where do you go? Do you uphold the character that God espouses for you, or does temptation overcome you?"

When no one is looking, when no one knows what you are doing, when you are at the best of who you are and when you are at your worst, what are you really like? A person's answers to these questions will paint a picture of his or her character, and a person's character inevitably shows itself through what he or she does.

The Quest for Character

Traditionally, people have defined themselves by what they are not or what they do not do. In his book *The Ca-*

nadians, Andrew H. Malcolm says that when the average
Canadian is asked, "What is a Canadian?" again and again
the most common response is, "We are not Americans!"
In general, Canadians have tended to identify themselves
by what they are not rather than articulate a statement of
their own national identity.[2] Christians have also given a
similar response when they describe themselves. When
asked, "What is a Christian?" the response is a list of
"nots" rather than a proactive compilation of what a
Christian *is*. Some churches have even made a practice of
defining a Christian by what a Christian does *not* do more
than by what a Christian *is*.

It is true that in the quest for holiness, we will want
to keep certain things away from us, because there are
things we should *not* do or be. More importantly, however, there are certain things that we will want to hold
on to—integrating them into our very beings. There
have been a lot of people throughout the history of
faith who have observed the approved "don't do" list
religiously, but they have not necessarily been the kind
of people who demonstrate Christlikeness. We need to
concentrate on what we *are* and *do* and stop worrying
about our reputations, because reputation is what people *think* we are. Character is what God *knows* we are.
The character God has in mind for us will permeate our
entire beings—there will be no need to worry about
reputation.

God is on a relentless quest to see character developed in His children in order for them to emulate
Christlikeness: the highest goal He desires for us. God
wants us to join Him in His quest, making it our own.
As emerging leaders learn what it means to merge their

desires with God's dream for them, they will also desire to pursue true character qualities in their lives.

Principles of Character

People frequently ask me, "You work with young leaders. What kind of leaders are emerging on the scene and what kind of leaders are going to lead the Church into the next century?" My answer is simple: "People of godly character." They may not be the most gifted, and the list of what they can't do may be a lot longer than the list of things they can do, but people of godly character are the ones who have what it takes to lead the Church.

Character can be wrapped up into actual principles of Christlikeness. We talk a lot about Christlikeness without talking about what those principles actually are.

Early on in Mark's Gospel Jesus says to the disciples, "Come, follow me . . . and I will make you fishers of men" (Mark 1:17). His first mission was to make disciples. He made this clear from the beginning. Our first principle, then, is that it is characteristic of Christlikeness to *have a passion and vision of passing on your faith.*

At times, we have a tendency to focus on the "nicer" aspects of Christlikeness, such as patience and kindness. These are valuable aspects of Christ's character, but we must realize that there is also a tough side to Christ. He didn't shy away from tough situations; instead, He stepped into them with authority. He came with authority because He knew God. *Authority* is a characteristic of Christlikeness.

Jesus also had *discernment* and, with that, He knew what people needed. Notice that sometimes, when He prayed for people, He prayed that their sins would be forgiven. Other times He prayed that they'd be healed, and yet other times He prayed that they'd experience a renewed life. He knew what they needed.

Discernment has three elements to it. The first part is being able to see beyond what the known world and your senses give you and knowing beyond what is knowable to human beings. The second part is knowing the difference between good and evil—such as the discerning of spirits or seeing into the dark side of the spiritual realm. The third aspect is made up of the ability to: 1) know the needs of a person and respond accordingly in a word of knowledge, wisdom, healing or even confrontation; 2) know not only what is *not* known to you but what to do with that information; and 3) speak the right words to the right person at the right time. Therefore, discernment is a spiritual wisdom that goes beyond what you can know on your own. It is a spiritually empowered way to penetrate the hearts and souls of other people.

In the mentoring relationship, individuals can be led through the following questions in order to evaluate their own character:

1. How will you live out your value system?
2. Are you a person with integrity?
3. Do you have a passion to pass on your faith?
4. Do you take hold of situations with authority?
5. Do you seek discernment?
6. Do you understand God's grace?
7. Do you hold yourself accountable to someone?
8. How does intentionality play out in your life?
9. Does your character reflect wholeness and honesty with congruence?

The Problem: Character Crisis

In 1985, when I was finishing seminary and beginning graduate school, I became fascinated with how to develop people through counseling and human resource courses. One question plagued me: How do you actually develop things like character? Being a good graduate student, I decided I would do a big literature search and find everything I could on character development.

I spent four hours in the university library and I came up with nothing. I thought, *I'm a lot worse at researching than I thought.* So I elicited help from three librarians, and in the next two hours we uncovered two books. Through all the interlibrary loan and computerized cataloging systems, we found two books that had been written on character development. Neither one had gone through more than one printing. They were that bad.

> When no one is looking, when you are at your best and when you are at your worst, what are you really like? A person's answer will paint a picture of his or her character.

I discovered that character development was "out." According to Stephen Covey's book *The Seven Habits of Highly Effective People*, prior to World War I, it was generally recognized that the best kind of people were those who had character. The success literature published in the United States from the late eighteenth century through World War I focuses on what Covey calls the "Character Ethic." Things like integrity, humility, fidelity, temperance, courage, justice, patience, industry, simplicity, modesty and the Golden Rule are included in this concept. It was nearly taken for granted in the North American context that, in developing effective people, the key was in the cultivation of their character. Emerging leaders would need to integrate certain principles and habits deep within their natures. Parents, educational institutions and churches knew it. Businesses knew that when they got sharp, young people they wanted to build into executives, it was necessary to show them not just *how* the organization worked, but the kind of person they had to *become* in order to contribute effectively.

However, Covey says, since World War I, we have taken on a Personality Ethic: "Dress for success. Get your colors done. Smile. Have a good attitude. Think big. Conquer your fears." My research seemed to indicate that between 1960 and 1985, the accepted approach to human development had become this: If you just do the right thing, in the right environment, and given the right experiences, then you will turn out the right kind of people. Rather than building the person's character from the inside out, the basic thrust became "quick-fix influence techniques, power strategies, communication skills, and positive attitudes."[3]

This kind of thinking has also crept into the Church. You get a new convert and what do you do? You tell that new believer what to do and what not to do—you clean up his lifestyle. "Read your Bible. Here are some study materials. Get the right cognitive input, think the right thoughts, do the right stuff and don't do the wrong stuff, and you'll be a great Christian. OK?"

Covey says that if society focuses solely on building a personality ethic (as ours has for the last fifty years), the negative implications will be huge. The 1980s have proven Covey to be a prophet. Take people in religion, business and government who were hot in the 1980s and look at them now. High percentages of them have fallen downhill, from televangelists to Donald Trump (although Trump has since risen back to popularity). Something has been missing in their lives—and in the lives of millions of people who aren't featured in the press. As a result, we are in the midst of a character crisis.

As a society we have bought into the humanistic behaviorism of our culture, and we have an awful lot of people sitting in church who—when people are looking—seem pretty good. But when no one is looking, they have missed the mark. People come to Christ with characters that are undernourished and deformed from years of maltreatment or neglect. If somebody does not help them process the hurt, the anger, the bitterness and the disappointments, they will sit in the pews of our churches year after year with either a huge, heavy spot or a huge, empty spot in their souls. They will not know what to do with it. A lot of great teaching and preaching will escape them.

How Character Formation Occurs

How does the transformation occur? What is changed? What are the outcomes? The development of godly character is about yielding control—*giving it up*—so that the Holy Spirit can accomplish His powerful work in the life of the individual. It is not about being better, doing more or trying harder. It takes more than adopting the right behaviors and receiving the right cognitive input to know real vibrancy in your life of faith. *It takes the power of God working in you.*

Paul states in Romans 8:29, "For those God foreknew he also predestined to be conformed to the likeness of his Son, that he might be the firstborn among many brothers." Behind these words is the concept of man's creation "in the image of God" (Genesis 1:27), as well as the thought of Christ being eternally the very image of God (see 2 Corinthians 4:4; Colossians 1:15). God is clearly working to take His beloved and adopted children and re-create them individually into the image of Christ, His Son.

Bill Hybels, in *Who You Are When No One's Looking*, describes how this change occurs:

> Christ's character is what God offers us when we timidly say we would like to be part of his family. Paul writes that those whom God chooses for his family members he makes "conformed to the image of his Son" (Rom. 8:29 [KJV])—he gives them character qualities like those of their elder brother, Jesus.
>
> He does this through the work of the Holy Spirit, his representative in our hearts. "We all . . . beholding . . . the glory of the Lord, are being changed into his likeness from one degree of glory to another; for this comes from the Lord who is the Spirit" (2 Cor. 3:18). The Spirit writes Jesus' own character traits on our hearts: "love, joy, peace, patience, goodness, faithfulness, gentleness, self-control" (Gal. 5:22-23).[4]

Character Formation Through Trial

Character is formed in us when we go through the most difficult moments of life. James 1:2-5 says,

> Count it all joy, my brothers and sisters, when you face many kinds of trials, because you know that the testing of your faith develops perseverance. Perseverance must finish its work that you may be mature and complete, lacking in nothing. If anyone lacks wisdom, ask God and He will give it generously to you. (author paraphrase)

James sees a direct link between the tough moments of life and faith and the development of true Christian character and maturity. He urges believers to *intentionally embrace difficult times in life.*

In a nearly parallel passage, Paul writes:

> Not only so, but we also rejoice in our sufferings, because we know that suffering produces perseverance; perseverance, character; and character, hope. And hope does not disappoint us, because God has poured out his love into our hearts by the Holy Spirit. (Romans 5:3-5)

Although Paul and James seldom sound parallel, the essence of their teaching is similar on this point. When the difficult moments come, whether these are the typical moments of life or divinely appointed disciplines, our personal response to them reflects our character and willingness to allow God to work even in the tough moments of life. What results from embracing trials are qualitative traits of character and a "perfecting" of the individual person. What actually develops is twofold: 1) the character of Christ and 2) individual character qualities such as perseverance and steadfastness.

A little over a year ago, I took a walk with my mother along a beach in California. As we walked, I asked her, "If you could, as my mother, take anything out of my life, I bet it's the following: Dad's death when I was fifteen, the farming accident when I was run over by a loaded hay wagon (with three tons of hay on it) when I was twenty and the virus I caught on an airplane five years ago which led to a three-year battle with chronic fatigue. If you, being my mother, could change anything in my life, you would take those away from me. Wouldn't you?" She nodded her head in agreement. I went on, "But if I am of any use to God today, it is probably because of those trials. They've made a tremendous difference." They helped form a life of character and a submission to Him.

> As emerging leaders learn what it means
> to merge their desires with God's dream
> for them, they will also desire to pursue
> true character qualities in their lives.

How is a Christian to respond in tribulation and sufferings? Our first response is to embrace them as a natural part of the journey to glory. It was true for Christ; it is the same for Christians. Do not hide from suffering; it will come, so embrace it! Second, while suffering leads ultimately to glory, it leads to maturity now. One does not learn endurance without suffering, because without it there would be little to endure. It is our personal response that makes the difference. Endurance over time builds solid character, as long as we respond with faith and hope rather than with resentment and bitterness. Faith and hope, then, is our third response. Sufferings keep our faith alive and our hope squarely on Him.

The response to tough times should not be, "Oh, good, another one!" This is not martyrdom. It is character formation. The mentoring relationship can allow God to work in individuals to conform them to the image of Christ in the midst of the difficult moments.

Intentional Formation

Character formation should also be intentional on the individual's part. We can't just wait for those big moments to come, like surfers can't just wait for that perfect wave. They ride the smaller waves too. They practice and have fun, and when the big one comes it does not take them by surprise. Our reactions to the mundane events in our lives are just as important in relation to character formation as our responses to the major events are.

Intentional character development involves small, routine decisions, like how we spend our time every day. When you have a three-day weekend, do you play cards, go to the movies, stay up late with your friends, read three more books or spend every afternoon going on long walks, listening to God? There are no right or wrong answers here. Sometimes you need to have fun. Sometimes you need to read books. And sometimes you need to go for walks with God. But realize that the decisions you make affect the kind of person you become.

Intentional development does take some planning. We have to start where we are now, see where we want to go and figure out what steps are needed for us to get there. Otherwise, the faithful mode of self-sufficiency will take over. We'll begin to think, *I haven't screwed up.*

I am doing pretty well. I have made it through another year. The mentoring relationship can be an aid in noticing a lack of intentional development and assessing the situation. I do not mean to imply a constant, morbid introspection, but young leaders must be careful not to let themselves slide through life on autopilot.

Character formation also demands planning for how individuals will deal with frustrations, quitting points and disappointments. I was teaching a course on pastoral theology for people who were going to minister overseas. There were two students in the class who were dealing with major disappointments and failures. One's wife had moved out that semester. The other was just beginning his seminary education after being fired from his first two churches—not a good start to ministry. During the final oral exam I asked both of them, in front of the other thirty students, "How are you going to deal with your current disappointment in a way that will allow God to build His character in you, so that five years from now you will be useful to Him?"

Their responses were worth more than any lecture I could have given. It made many of the students think about their own decisions. Young leaders need to consider what they are going to do with disappointments. They can become bitter, they can feel hurt and they can blame, or they can turn the disappointments into opportunities to grow in grace, have a deeper understanding and empathy and exude Christlikeness.

Another part of intentionally developing character is dealing with our dark sides. We all have one. Don't lie to yourself or to anyone else—it is there. It may be the size of a thumbnail or it may be the whole other half of who you are. Either way, if individuals do not maintain a firm control over it, before long it will start to take over and it will devour them. It happens very, very subtly. A mentor can help young leaders clearly identify their dark sides and face them. There is something powerful about articulating, exposing and confessing your dark side so that at least one other person—and God—hears.

In the mentoring process, the significance of helping each other along the journey of life is one of the biggest principles of spiritual development I know. I cannot show you one person making major strides in Christlikeness who is doing it alone. He or she is doing it in a relationship with at least one other person. It is important for mentorees to find a place where people pray for and nurture them, listen to them, know their dark sides and ask them about them. And it is important for mentorees to answer the mentors honestly. God works powerfully in such a setting to conform people into the image of His Son.

Character Counts

The emerging biblical pattern of character development seen thus far has four distinct principles. The first involves the individual's response to the difficulties of life (see Romans 5:3-5 and James 1:2-5). These include internal and external temptations; the frustrations, humiliations and disappointments of life; and the trials and persecutions that come from living a distinctively Christian life in a world that expresses constant opposition to that way of life.

The second principle espouses the more mundane but constant, personal involvement of consistent, daily growth in godly character. James and Paul call this perseverance. This is also what Moses demonstrated during those forty years of leading the Israelites in the wilderness. This kind of perseverance is what allowed Joshua to be Moses' assistant for those forty years and still have the faith, strength and vision to finally lead his people into Canaan and the land of promise. This perseverance is a daily decision to embrace the faith, values and life-changing character qualities that bring about transformational development.

The third principle involves the work of the Holy Spirit, who accomplishes developmental transformation from the inside out (see Romans 8:28-29; 2 Corinthians 3:18). Here, the Holy Spirit does the work of chiseling, perfecting, enlightening and transforming; in essence, He develops the actual character of Christ deep within the heart and life of the willing Christian.

The fourth principle involves the willing responses of the individual. Transformational development is not an easy road. Eugene Peterson called it "a long obedience in the same direction."[5] It involves personal choice, commitment, perseverance and a willful decision to follow. The result is an intimate relationship with God, the inner working of the Holy Spirit conforming the individual internally and externally to the image of Christ and a life of significance, character and integrity.

In the mentoring process, the focus on character development is crucial in the life of the emerging leader. In character-based leadership development, the mentoree focuses on Christlike character formation as a foundation for life and ministry not only in the early years but throughout life. God delights to show His power in the lives of people. His great goal and plan in history is that we as His children reflect the image of Jesus Christ. The result is people of godly character, people He uses.

In *The Quest for Character*, Chuck Swindoll writes,

> God is forever on a quest. Ever thought about that? His pursuit is a subject woven through the fabric of the New Testament. The pattern He follows is set forth in Romans 8:29, where He promises to conform us to His Son's image. Another promise is stated in Philippians 1:6, where we're told He began His work in us and He isn't about to stop. Elsewhere He even calls us His "workmanship" (Ephesians 2:10). He is hammering, filing, chiseling, and shaping us! Peter's second letter goes so far as to *list* some of the things included in this quest—diligence, faith, moral excellence, knowledge, self-control, perseverance, godliness, kindness, and love (2 Peter 1:5-7). In a word . . . character.
>
> Character qualities in His children—that's God's relentless quest. His strobe light will continue to penetrate our darkness. He won't quit His quest until He completes His checklist. And when will that be? When we rest in peace . . . and not one day sooner. Only then will His mission be accomplished in us. We have Him to thank for not giving up as we go through the process of developing character.[6]

It is up to us to join Him in that quest for Christlikeness at the core of our very beings. As God works His will in emerging young leaders, they can know the humbling joy of hearing those closest to them begin to say, "You know, you remind me of Someone. You are an awful lot like Him. There's a striking resemblance."

Key Thoughts from This Chapter

1. God's dream is to conform each believer to the very image of Christ (see Romans 8:29). The mentoring process assists in making that dream an actual reality.
2. Character involves:
   a. Passion and vision
   b. Authority
   c. Discernment
3. In times of character crisis in society, government and business, it will require people of godly character to lead the Church in this century.
4. Character is formed in the lives of leaders through:
   a. Responses to life's toughest challenges
   b. Intentional patterns and life decisions that build character traits into one's life
5. Character can be intentionally formed through:
   a. Making small, routine decisions
   b. Planning for frustrations, quitting points and disappointments
   c. Dealing with one's dark side

Questions for Further Reflection

1. Begin to identify specific things God has used to conform you to the image of Christ. Has the pattern been more through events, crises or memorable experiences, or more by intentional patterns of your life and key decisions you have made?
2. Begin to dream about what your character could look like when you reflect the holiness, charac-

ter, humility and righteousness of Christ in your daily life. What adjustments need to be made or patterns need to be developed in order for you to fulfill that dream?

Action Plan

1. Begin to identify any character issues that you need to address in your life. Ask a close friend or family member to help you identify these.
2. Initiate a pattern of prayer and honestly addressing these character traits to be developed and character flaws to be addressed.

Notes

1. Charles R. Swindoll, *The Quest for Character: Inspirational Thoughts for Becoming More Like Christ* (Portland: Multnomah, 1987), p. 54.
2. Andrew H. Malcolm, *The Canadians* (Toronto: PaperJacks Ltd., 1985), n.p.
3. Stephen R. Covey, *The Seven Habits of Highly Effective People: Powerful Lessons in Personal Change* (New York: Simon and Schuster, 1990), pp. 18-9.
4. Bill Hybels, *Who You Are When No One's Looking: Choosing Consistency, Resisting Compromise* (Downers Grove, IL: InterVarsity Press, 1987), pp. 111-2.
5. Eugene Peterson, *A Long Obedience in the Same Direction: Discipleship in an Instant Society* (Downers Grove, IL: InterVarsity Press, 1980), n.p.
6. Swindoll, *The Quest for Character*, p. 14.

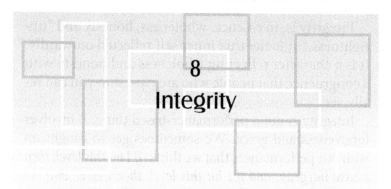

8
Integrity

WHEN YOU THINK ABOUT integrity, what kinds of words or expressions come to mind? Do you think of words like *ethics, punctuality, consistency, honesty, sincerity* or *conviction*? Dr. D. James Kennedy describes integrity as falling under the larger umbrella of character.

> In a person, character includes those habits and personality traits that distinguish us as individuals, especially in regard to personal integrity, courage, moral fiber, and individual initiative.[1]

Character in this context begins to wrap together not just who you are but *how your value systems are actually lived out.* This is integrity.

The word *integrity* appears in the Bible a number of times. In its Hebrew root form, it means, literally, that you are a person of substance.[2] You are the person you say you are. This denotes authenticity rather than a veneer. With veneer you have some sort of cheap wood underneath but a nice covering that makes it look good. Integrity is the exact opposite. What you present yourself to be, you are *clear through.* What you see is what you get; what you say is what you are; what you project yourself to be is what you deliver.

Integrity is, in essence, wholeness, honesty and "up-rightness." It is the true inner self reflected outwardly. It is a character reflecting wholeness and honesty with a congruence that people who are closest to you can really see.

Integrity is not a performance-based thing. It involves forgiveness and grace. We sometimes get so caught up with our performances that we think, *If I hit this level, then I have integrity, and if I hit this level, then I enter into the realms of holiness.* Integrity does not focus on performance. There is not a measuring stick by which you can maintain integrity or holiness. It is all simply by the grace of God. And it is essential in the life of a young leader.

Integrity in the Life of David

Psalm 51 provides a good example of integrity lived out. David, the great king of Israel, was in the center of the action. He was a man of passion. He loved his God, and he loved serving as king of God's people. He loved all of his wives, and he was a great family man.

At the same time, David also had a dark side. In this sense, we can all identify with him. His struggles with that very real dark side of his soul led to a chain of events that have become exceedingly well-known. David was quite taken with Bathsheba, and they spent the evening together. Later, David found out that Bath-sheba had conceived a child, and he had to figure out what to do about it. Things kept getting more and more complicated, and David found himself involved in a murder plot—a successful one. He tried desperately to figure out how to cover up all of his sin, all of the poor decisions he had made. Finally, one of God's prophets,

Nathan, came to David and said, in effect, "David, forget it, man. Come back to God. It's the only way to go." David realized the truth of what Nathan was saying. He could not go on any longer the way things were.

Psalm 51 is the record of David's cry for renewal in his relationship with God. In verse 1, he prays, "Have mercy on me, O God,/ according to your unfailing love;/ according to your great compassion/ blot out my transgressions."

> David understood something that we've all missed at some point in our lives: Integrity doesn't mean that we will never mess up. Integrity means that we deal honestly with our mess-ups.

God's "unfailing love" is the key to this whole psalm. The New American Standard translation of the Bible talks about God's lovingkindness. It's a great word, one of the strongest words in all of the Old Testament. Lovingkindness literally involves the idea of a covenant or a contract. God says, "Let's agree to a covenant—you and Me. I want you. I want your life. I want everything you are and everything you will be. In return, I will give you everything I've got." Furthermore, God so obligates Himself to us that He literally says, "I'm never leaving." That's what lovingkindness means. By saying yes to God and His covenant, we appropriate His power, strength and resources. He makes them available to us, but it's up to us to take hold of them.

As we seek to find restoration and renewal in the very presence of God, this verse can be the cry of our hearts as well. David had chosen his words carefully. They teach us much about how to "just say yes" to God.

Dealing Honestly with the Soul

In the next few verses of Psalm 51, David prays,

> Wash away all my iniquity
>   and cleanse me from my sin.
>
> For I know my transgressions,
>   and my sin is always before me.
> Against you, you only, have I sinned
>   and done what is evil in your sight. (51:2-4)

When I first examined this psalm, my initial reaction to David's words was, "Come on, Dave! Cut to the chase, will you? What is this—'my iniquity'? 'My transgressions'? Dave, you messed up big. Let's call it what it is. You sinned! You sinned in the worst way. And you did it again and again. Then you covered it up, lied about it and killed somebody! It doesn't get worse than this." It really doesn't! David's life was a mess at this point.

After reading through the passage a few more times, however, I began to see a few things that I hadn't seen the first time through. I discovered the awesomeness of the word *iniquity*. It refers to something good, healthy and right that's been twisted just enough to become unhealthy, improper and wrong. David was a man of passion. He felt everything deeply. He loved his God deeply. He loved everything deeply. David's love was a good thing—a very good thing that was healthy and right—except he gave it a twist, just a little twist, and it became wrong. That's iniquity.

Have you ever noticed how caring for someone can shift just a little, and love turns to lust, desire turns to control, and dreams turn to anger? You take a boat out on the lake, and you're enjoying great recreation. Then something leaks, and recreation turns to disaster. In the same way, good things about you can become twisted just a little and turn into iniquities.

Most of us think we're not incredibly terrible people. We don't consider the song "Bad to the Bone" as a theme for our lives. However, all of us have the ability to take something that is good and twist it ever so slightly. You can take something that is beautiful, healthy and good and twist it into something that devours your soul a little at a time.

It is important for us to be honest and have perspective when it comes to integrity in our lives, because it is very easy for us to deceive ourselves. The mentoring relationship can be key in providing this perspective.

Understanding Grace

In Psalm 26:1, David, standing on a platform and looking like a prophet, says, "Vindicate me, O LORD, for I have walked in my integrity" (NASB). And throughout Psalm 51 he talks about integrity. Reading these verses, I want to argue, "Dave, I don't think you should be the national spokesperson for integrity. OK, let's play a game. Does the name *Bathsheba* mean anything to you? Let's try another one: *Uriah*. Does that name mean anything to you? Which word doesn't fit: *David, Bathsheba, Uriah* or *Integrity*? Which word doesn't fit here, Dave? Come on—play along with me. Which word doesn't fit?"

But David understood something that I was missing, what we've all missed at some point in our lives: Integrity doesn't mean that we will *never* mess up. That is why God offers us things like communion and forgiveness. Integrity means that we have permission to mess up within the limitations of boundaries, and when we do mess up, we deal *honestly* with it. We don't hide it from God, we don't hide it from ourselves, and we don't hide it from anyone else. Don't miss this point. Integrity is the *intentionality* of dealing with our lives with absolute honesty.

> God wants to use us. He doesn't desire a bigger, deeper, better commitment. He just wants willing spirits that at every turn say, "Yes! Yes!" to Him.

When David comes to the point of dealing honestly with himself and he realizes the enormity of what he has done, his response is, "Lord, make me clean. Make me absolutely as clean as you can. I want to be a person of absolute cleanliness" (see 51:7, 9). Because of his mistakes, being a person of integrity would have been pretty difficult for David. He had been exposed to the entire nation, not just to a few people who knew him well. Yet, after he was restored and renewed, he wanted to be a man of real integrity.

When young leaders find themselves in a spot in which they cannot follow through in absolute obedience and integrity, it does not have to be the end of the story—unless they *choose* for that to be the end of the story. If they repent and truly return to the Lord, there is sure to be restoration for them. There may be limitations placed on them because of their failure, but it is important for them to keep in mind that repentance is foundational to being a person of integrity. In order to have the kind of life David is talking about here, we have to deal honestly with our mistakes and take our barriers down and open our hearts. We must say, "God, make me clean. Clear through. I want to truly be what I show myself to be." It's a powerful prayer that says yes to all of God's power, grace and lovingkindness. Integrity reflects in us God's holiness, standards and grace.

Intentionality

For many people who've grown up in the Church, being a Christian is similar to personal hygiene. It's just something we do. We brush our teeth; we do devotions. It's like a morning ritual. We pride ourselves because we do it well and consistently—but we don't do it well for the right reasons. The intentionality of living out our faith has escaped us.

In the middle of Psalm 51, the text moves away from renewal to the willingness of the soul. David asks God to work in his life, but he does not leave the matter solely up to God. Furthermore, he's not just asking God; he's also putting himself into the picture and saying, "I'm willing to cooperate."

In verse 10, David says: "Create in me a pure heart, O God,/ and renew a steadfast spirit within me." The underlying issue is seeking a pure, clean heart from God—and keeping it. David isn't seeking renewal that will expire within a week or two. It's not a request for a temporary cleaning or a shot, something to sustain him until the next dose. He doesn't want something that will lose its effect over time. He's talking about an *intentional life of pu-*

rity and holiness. It's so easy for us to lose focus and settle back into neglect and self-protection instead of taking up our position in Christ every day—taking on the fullness of the Spirit, setting our eyes on Christ and walking in the light. David desires to be clean clear through *every day.*

Integrity doesn't mean just *doing* the right things; it means *intentionally thinking through* what you do. A mentor can lead young leaders to explore their motives and ask, "Why do I do the right things?" "How do I do the right things?" Some people think that if they do the right things then everything will be OK, but sometimes people do the right things for the wrong reasons. We need to figure out if we're doing the right thing because it's really a part of who we are or if we're just doing what we're supposed to do.

Accountability

Integrity often requires accountability. The odds of growing well in integrity and Christlikeness on our own are limited. It really requires being involved with another person who will ask direct questions and then listen. The mentor should build nurture into the relationship so that the mentoree's attitude does not become, "I have to do well or I will have to tell somebody all about my life—especially what I don't want to tell him." Accountability looks a lot different than simply retelling the events of our lives to another individual (see chapter 3).

Accountability and perspective go together. Often when we go through times in our lives that are difficult, the person we are accountable to can give us perspective. I have found that many people who have grown up in a Christian environment generally develop a narrow view. Something is either right or wrong, black or white. Talking to someone can give us perspective. Perspective can often lead to grace, when we can hear someone say, "I can see where you came up with that, but Christians around the world don't look at it that way. If you want to give yourself some grace, there is grace in this situation."

The real wisdom of the mentor is in knowing when to be direct and when to offer grace, or how to do both at appropriate times. When Nathan came to David, his role as the prophet was to help David objectively see the true state of his soul, what he had done and the implications of his actions. So much of mentoring is about accountability and perspective.

Saying Yes

Integrity. What I say is what I want to be. What I show is what I want to be clear through—a person of true integrity. Integrity is a crucial part of the mentoring relationship. Without it, the mentor and mentoree will be working toward an end without any means to hold it up. Your relationship will merely be a veneer with no substance.

In verse 12 of Psalm 51, David asks of God, "Sustain me with a willing spirit" (author paraphrase). You see, David knows himself. He knows his very real ability to mess up, even with the best of intentions. David knows he will make more mistakes, so he prays, "Lord, if I am going to keep this clean heart, this joy of salvation, if I am really going to do this right, You've got to uphold me with a willing spirit."

Notice that he is asking God to work with him. David has not forgotten the lovingkindness, that covenant, that contract, they made together back in verse 1. "Lord, work with me to accomplish this," David is saying. "Lord, make me willing to say yes to You at every turn."

Verse 16 says, "You do not delight in sacrifice, or I would bring it;/ you do not take pleasure in burnt offerings." David is saying, "I know, Lord, what You want. You don't want 'religious practice.' *You want me.*" Throughout the psalm, these words themselves encompass God's response. He says, "David, if you are willing, I am powerful and I am not leaving. You're my man, David. It's you and Me."

God wants us—not what we can do, not what we can give. He wants who we are at our best and worst. He already knows the dark sides of our souls. He knows those iniquities deep within. Think of the number of people in the Bible who messed up really big. God still used some of them because they dealt honestly with what they had done.

God wants to use us. He doesn't desire a bigger, deeper, better commitment. He doesn't even want more or deeper repentance. He just wants us and our willing spirits that at every turn and every moment say, "Yes! Yes!" to Him. Not, "Let me think it through," or "Maybe tomorrow," or "I'll work on that." It's "Yes!" at every turn.

Verse 17 offers a model for saying yes: "The sacrifices of God are a broken spirit;/ a broken and contrite heart,/ O God, you will not despise." This is what the Bible calls a "living" sacrifice that regularly says yes to God and leads to a life that He can use. We can learn from David's example. We can take our deeper understanding of integrity and all that it entails, together with David's example of integrity in a life after huge mistakes, and tie it all together by saying yes to God!

Key Thoughts from This Chapter

1. Integrity is your essence—the true inner self reflected outwardly. It is not performance-based, however. It involves forgiveness and grace.

2. David understood something we have all missed at some point in our lives: Integrity does not mean that we will never mess up. Integrity means that we deal honestly with our mess-ups.

3. If mentoring is intentionally developing the next generation of emerging leaders, then in the mentoring process, integrity means intentionally thinking through who we are and what we do.

4. Integrity requires accountability, being involved with another person who will hold us accountable.

Questions for Further Reflection

1. Which aspect of integrity from the definitions and descriptions in this chapter struck you the most? Explain why.

2. When you ask God to "create in [you] a pure heart" (Psalm 51:10), what aspect of your life do you have to repeatedly seek His forgiveness for in order to keep your heart pure? Do you understand why?

3. What does a willing spirit look like for you?

Action Plan

1. Identify what integrity will look like in your life. Decide what aspects of your life will require accountability, more grace, time to resolve or even someone to confront you.

Notes

1. D. James Kennedy, *Character and Destiny: A Nation in Search of Its Soul* (Grand Rapids: Zondervan, 1994), p. 193.
2. Stephen L. Carter, *Integrity* (New York: HarperCollins, 1996), p. 19.

9

Dealing with the Private, Deeper Issues

SOMETIMES IT IS A challenge to know what to do with all the experiences, problems, temptations, successes and failures that come our way—especially the big or nagging ones. A significant concept in counseling and human development is the idea of *processing*, or working through an issue in a way that allows individuals to understand a problem's dimensions, power, impact and even its purpose in their lives. But it is a challenge to do this on one's own. The mentoring relationship can be a safe and useful place to talk through some of these issues. This chapter offers several exercises to help individuals process the issues of life and the soul within the context of the mentoring relationship.

Dealing with Private "Stuff"

As leaders emerge and move toward a place of significance, it is often desirable and helpful for them to work through some key issues of personal development. The personal dimensions of the issues vary greatly, but at the core the issues are similar. Whether they are about personal security or insecurities, sexuality or fantasies of significance, they are often issues that can be initially addressed with a mentor based on the relationship's trust and safety.

Although this is often a preferred method for the emerging leader to deal with personal issues, exposing one's innermost thoughts and feelings with another individual can be a significant threat to both mentor and mentoree. For the mentoree, it can be intimidating. Yet, at the same time, the experience can be both highly desirable and profitable. For many, sharing these private issues with the mentor is often the first time another person (particularly a trusted, older authority figure) has ever heard the individual's story and seen his or her fears, dark side or insecurities.

Key issues of personal development, such as security and insecurities, sexuality or fantasies of significance, are often issues that can be addressed with a mentor based on the relationship's trust and safety.

On the other hand, the mentor may feel uncomfortable listening to these private thoughts and may also feel a great responsibility to "fix" the issues or solve the problem. But that is not the role of the mentor. Rather, the mentor's role is to be the trusted person who demonstrates wisdom and listens, responds with assurance and prays. In many mentoring relationships, this level of communication will serve as the foundation for in-depth forms of communication that can foster not only a healthy relationship but new levels of emotional and spiritual development for both parties.

People have used this kind of confession process throughout history. In the earliest days of the Church, in the first and second centuries, people openly confessed their sins, according to James 5:16. For centuries in the Roman Catholic Church, priests have heard confessions and offered absolution to the truly repentant. Within the Protestant Church confession is a private, spiritual exercise between the individual believer and God. It can also be a healthy experience to articulate a confession to a mentor or a trusted friend. In so doing, a person can break the power of the Enemy's accusations and feel freed of the sins or patterns that have trapped him or her. For these unique situations I use an exercise called "A Confession of Your Life."

Exercise: "A Confession of Your Life"

In this exercise, the individual will ask two or three friends to meet with him or her for at least two hours. Included in the group should be a close, trusted friend, a mentor and a person who is spiritually discerning. The friend is there to give assurance and be a kind face—someone with whom the individual feels safe. The mentor is there simply as a resource person to give insight, prayer or an appropriate word. The third person should have a good deal of spiritual discernment, know at what point it's appropriate to break any spiritual stronghold that the Enemy may have gained and be able to pray appropriate prayers that may surround spiritual bondage, if any is present.

The purpose of the exercise is simply to walk through the individual's life from beginning to end, working through a confession of sin and life experiences and processing any issues that emerge that still hold power over the person's heart or mind. Although the individual may be keenly aware of the positional forgiveness of his or her sin, the ability to experience real forgiveness and consequently to be able to move on can be missing in his or her life. This exercise seems to give people a very simple structure from which they can move past some issues that have otherwise held them back in their development.

Working through "A Confession of Your Life" is certainly not a requirement for every person; after all, who would look forward to doing this? But this exercise has been used many times to help break through issues in people's pasts and bring an inner release where it has never been before. The exercise has proven to be highly effective from an experiential learning perspective for many young leaders in their developmental process. It helps them deal with some of the inner and private issues that have come up again and again, which they seemingly have not been able to put behind them. This exercise enables people to put their "stuff" in their pasts so they can move on developmentally.

Dealing with Past "Stuff"

Past "stuff" consists of issues from our pasts that continue to plague our development and are best processed with a trusted friend (and, if necessary, through follow-up with a professional counselor or therapist). However, as we are describing it, past stuff can be something that occurs from birth on up, and that continues to limit growth throughout all of the developmental stages of life.

Past stuff is not necessarily sin to be confessed or issues that need to be addressed in counseling. Rather, it is about *perceptions and perspectives*. It is about things said to us or about us that still stick in our minds. It is about how we felt or were made to feel about ourselves, particularly as we sought to relate to those around us. It is about subconscious thoughts or feelings that we have embraced as true but have actually never thought through, processed or evaluated as adults.

It is not unusual to find young leaders in a seminary class or seminar who seem very capable and gifted. Yet, after a brief conversation and a few questions, these talented young leaders confess significant doubts, fears, insecurities or other unprocessed "stuff." The question they most often ask is, "What do I do with this stuff?" The following exercise helps process these issues so that growth in deficient areas can occur.

Exercise: "Guided Prayer Time"

In this exercise, the intent is to invite the Holy Spirit to work through the individual and for the individual to submit to God's will. Set aside two or more hours for this exercise. There should typically be two resource people present: a trusted friend and support person and a spiritual director. Begin the exercise with prayer, simply stating that the individual desires to belong completely to God and to get rid of any issues in his or her life that are in the way of the Holy Spirit's ability to conform him or her to the image of Christ. The individual must yield to the Holy Spirit so that only the things that are important from His perspective will come to mind; this will give the Spirit the freedom to accomplish His complete purpose. Ask the Holy Spirit to specifically address issues of character and personal development that in any way place barriers on the individual's spiritual formation.

The spiritual director will then make a series of commands about the spiritual realms. First, he or she will limit any authority or power the spiritual world may have gained access to in the individual's life at any point in the past. Next, the director will command that all spiritual forces are in complete submission to the Holy Spirit and to this process because of the shed blood and resurrection of the Lord Jesus Christ. After the commands have been made, the leader will simply state that the individual wants to belong completely to Christ, that he or she asks the Holy Spirit to come and lead the individual back through his or her life, starting with the earliest days of childhood and bringing to mind anything that is a barrier in development or conformation.

Typically, a person's life will be segmented into four parts, beginning with the first five years of life and ending with the young adult years. The key is to simply ask the Holy Spirit to bring to mind anything that has placed limitations on the individual's development, anything said to or about him or her, any abuses, anything that has left an emotional, psychological or spiritual scar in the first five years of his or her life. Then repeat the same process, asking the Holy Spirit to cover ages six through twelve. The leader will then ask the Spirit: 1) to stand with the individual at age twelve; 2) to pronounce those first twelve years of his or her life holy and given over completely to God; and 3) that any issues present be bundled up and removed, forgiven and buried in the depths of the sea to be remembered no more.

After these steps are completed, the leader will move to the next stage in the individual's life and ask the

Holy Spirit to lead him or her through the teenage years. The group will deal with issues of identity, sexuality and abuse (either being a recipient of abuse or ways the individual has hurt or abused other people). Then ask the Holy Spirit to bring absolute forgiveness and restoration and to pronounce the teen years holy and given over completely to God.

After you have covered the teen years, walk through the college years and cover the same issues (identity, direction, value, poor decisions made, etc.). Make the same requests of the Spirit to bring forgiveness and restoration. Depending on the individual's age, you may need to repeat the requests and prayers in order to deal with the post-college years.

> The goal is to keep all of life in perspective. A mentor can be that trusted person who assists in processing life and its experiences.

When you have gone through all of the life stages, ask the Holy Spirit to take all of the issues that surfaced from the early childhood, teen and young adult years, remove them from the individual and bring absolute forgiveness. Then, the leader will ask the Spirit to identify the individual's biological parents and break any unhealthy spiritual holds that have come from either side of the family, going several generations back. To close the prayer time, the leader will simply ask the Holy Spirit if there's anything else that needs to be addressed.

Then, make the following requests: First, ask the Holy Spirit to come and purify the individual's mind and heart. Next, ask that the individual be filled completely with His presence and power. Finally, ask that the individual be able to take his or her full position in Christ and understand what it means to be a holy and dearly loved child of God.

The significance of the guided prayer time varies from person to person, but most find it beneficial to go through the process of simply yielding control to the Holy Spirit. Quite often individuals report significant breakthroughs where the power of the past, old memories and even compulsive patterns is diminished or completely erased.

Dealing with Unprocessed "Stuff"

For some emerging leaders, the issues in their lives are not primarily private or tied to the past. Rather, they have some stuff that is just *left over*—unprocessed. In our quest to be the most effective, fully devoted followers of Christ possible, it is useful for us to process this leftover "stuff." Whether the issues are emotional, spiritual, psychological or developmental, it is fairly simple to process them. Think of this in the same way that we deal with the leftover physical stuff in our lives.

Exercise: "Closet Analogy"

One way to deal with leftovers is to use the closet analogy. Remember when you were growing up and your parents made you clean out all of the old stuff in your closet? You would spend the day taking each thing out, reflecting on it and bringing back memories. You looked at each item and asked, "Do I want to keep this? Why do I want to keep this? What will I do with this? Does it still fit me? Is it still a part of me?" By the end of the day you would have pitched some significant things. You also would have kept a few things, but you would know why you kept them and would recognize their significance.

You can use this analogy to help the individual *mentally* process his or her leftover stuff. He or she will take the leftover issues, one at a time, out of the mental closet and decide if he or she wants to keep or dispose of them. He or she should ask what they are worth, why he or she should keep them or what benefits there are to getting rid of them. He or she will proceed through the entire mental closet until it looks neatly organized, with its items arranged in orderly rows, "mental shoes" lined up on the floor beside each other and the boxes on the top shelf sorted and stacked neatly on top of each other.

The key is for the individual to look at the issues of his or her life and past and *process* the leftover mental "stuff" so that he or she is aware of what is there and what it means. Encourage the individual to look at what has happened to him or her and figure out why he or she is the way he or she is. See if it's still true or if it is just a leftover or unprocessed perspective that needs to be pitched.

"How Old Are You in Your Mind?"

In the same way that fashion, computer technology or communication styles have to be updated, so do perceptions of one's self, role, function and being. One of the key questions I ask emerging leaders is, "How old are you in your mind?" The responses are revealing and often quite useful.

It is not unusual for young leaders in their twenties to say that when they take a good look at themselves they still think of themselves as being much younger, even when others see them as mature and competent. We often hear from young men in particular that they see themselves on the same level developmentally as a junior high- or early high school-aged boy. They do not see themselves in any way as emerging young leaders and men. It is also not unusual to listen to older, developing leaders in their mid-thirties to late forties who identify themselves on the same level developmentally as teenagers or college-aged men. When people respond this way, you can take that opportunity to explore the "stuff" in their lives that is unprocessed by using one or more of the exercises in this chapter.

Updating and Moving Ahead

As we move through the developmental stages of our lives, faith and ministries, it is intriguing to see how many things change. The goal is to keep all of life in *perspective*. A mentor can be that trusted person who assists in processing life and its experiences. Throughout this chapter we have explored a series of exercises to assist us in processing both past issues and current perspectives. Our spiritual lives flourish best when our confessions are kept current and we "walk in the light" (1 John 1:7) and "walk in the Spirit" (see Galatians 5:16). It is also true that we flourish emotionally and spiritually when our perspectives of life, ministry and ourselves are current.

It should be noted that these exercises are not intended to replace traditional counseling or therapy for those who need it, but to serve as tools within the mentoring relationship for those who want or need perspective in their lives. When some new perspective is gained, many feel empowered in their spirits to move ahead in greater effectiveness for the cause of Christ.

Key Thoughts from This Chapter

1. Mentorees need to begin working through any issues of their lives that could potentially limit their development in the mentoring process.
2. In this chapter, three approaches and exercises are described to aid you in dealing with private issues:
   a. A Confession of Your Life
   b. Guided Prayer Time
   c. Closet Analogy
3. Mentorees should be encouraged to update their lives, leftover issues, emotional development and "age in their minds" so that there is a congruence in their lives, minds and souls.

Questions for Further Reflection

1. In your mentoring relationship(s), is it more challenging for you or the other person to discuss the most private issues of your life?
2. Is it time to do an "absolute confession of your life" to someone? If you have already done it, describe to your mentor(s) how or why it was useful.
3. Are you aware of any doubts, fears or leftover "stuff" that you would like to leave behind? Which of the described exercises might be most useful to you?

4. How old are you in your mind? Describe how you will begin to narrow the gap between your chronological age and your age in your mind.

Action Plan

1. Create a two- to five-step action plan for updating any of the deeper, private or unresolved issues of your life.

10
Developing Healthy Emotional and Spiritual Sides of Life and Ministry

Feeding the Emotional Side

IN THE MENTORING PROCESS, it is essential to deal with issues of both spiritual *and* emotional health. Historically, more emphasis has been placed upon spiritual health and little time has been given to dealing honestly with and building a healthy emotional aspect in individuals' lives and ministries.

Bill Hybels, pastor of Willow Creek Community Church in South Barrington, Illinois, has written an article and presented seminars for pastors on how to read the gauges of their lives. He states that often we check the physical gauge and make sure we're getting enough exercise and taking care of our physical bodies. We also have a spiritual gauge that we read to evaluate how well we're doing in that area. But often the emotional gauge is neglected; it is often not even considered. Before Hybels realized the emotional part of his own exhaustion, he chalked it up to spiritual matters. But he discovered something different when he experienced a particularly exhausting period in his ministry.

> "Did I get enough out of the Word of God as I needed? Did I pray? Did I fast? Did I prepare? Was I accurate? Did the elders affirm the message? Have I

kept to my diet? Have I been working out? Yes, I must be okay. Buck up! Let's go, Bill!" Since these spiritual and physical gauges—the only two on my dashboard—consistently signal "go," I have pushed myself as hard and as fast as possible. But recently a different part of my engine began to misfire.[1]

> Many of the problems related to emotional exhaustion could be dealt with if leaders were given better resources for developing emotional health.

As a result of our neglect of the emotional gauge, many people in ministry find themselves spiritually "low." Terms such as *stress, burnout* and even *depression* emerge. Archibald Hart, former dean of the Graduate School of Psychology at Fuller Theological Seminary, wrote in *Theology, News and Notes*:

> There is much ignorance in both secular and religious circles about the emotions or how humans function, even in these modern days. Those who serve the church, then, need wholesome, truthful education in these matters. And who are better equipped to do this than the products of our seminary-based education? Evangelicals tend also to sweep significant emotional problems under the rug. Many devout Christians receive no treatment whatsoever for serious emotional disorders because they are either afraid of the stigmatizations associated with such treatment or they have been taught to spiritualize their emotional problems and seek relief only through a greater effort at piety.[2]

Many of the problems related to emotional exhaustion could be dealt with if leaders were given better resources for developing emotional health. In the mentoring process it is absolutely essential to deal with these issues if the next generation is going to develop a whole, balanced approach to life and ministry.

Description and Evaluation of Emotional Exhaustion

Symptoms	Description
Fatigue	A sense of being drained; burnout
Avoidance, withdrawal	A result of extensive emotional output over an extended period of time
Negative thinking, forgetfulness, irritability	Inadequate emotional input for the amount of output that is required
An assortment of stomach and other stress-related ailments	A feeling that everyone wants more from you than you are able to give; a sense of inadequacy, failure or frustration; hurt or anger

Bear in mind what I mean by living in an emotionally depleted state. Emotional exhaustion is the utter depletion of a God-given energy resource. It is not another name for stress, depression or burnout, but it certainly includes these issues in varying degrees with respect to each person.

Note the following definitions of burnout and stress and their contrasts:

Burnout	Stress
A defense characterized by disengagement	Characterized by over-engagement
Emotions become blunted	Emotions become over-reactive
Emotional damage is primary	Physical damage is primary
Exhaustion affects motivation and drive	Exhaustion affects physical energy
Produces demoralization	Produces disintegration
Can be best understood as a loss of ideals and hope	Can be best understood as a loss of fuel and energy
Depression is caused by the grief engendered by the loss of ideals and hope	Depression is produced by the body's need to protect itself and conserve energy
Produces a sense of helplessness and hopelessness	Produces a sense of urgency and hyperactivity
Produces paranoia, depersonalization and detachment	Produces panic and phobic and anxiety-type disorders
May never kill you, but your long life may not seem worth living	May kill you prematurely, and you won't have enough time to finish what you started[3]

Emotional Exhaustion Inventory

In my own development as a pastor, I have found my self-awareness to be lacking. For example, I may perceive my ministry on any given day to be doing fine. My wife, however, might see me displaying frustration or anger on that very same day. When she scrutinizes me, inevitably her analysis of my emotional state is more accurate than my own. That's why I have found exercises like the following inventory, "Red Flags of Emotional Exhaustion," which was designed by Archibald Hart, to be helpful. The inventory has been modified from its original form for the purposes of this book. Its intention is to help define and identify a person's emotional condition.

> Review the past twelve months of your total life-work, social situation, family and recreation. Reflect on each of the following questions and rate the amount of change that has occurred during this period. Place more emphasis on change that has occurred during the past six months.
>
> Use the following scale and assign a number to each question that reflects the degree of change you have experienced. Be honest; the value of this self-assessment is negligible if you don't!
>
> 1 No or little change
> 2 Just noticeable change
> 3 Noticeable change
> 4 Fair degree of change
> 5 Great degree of change

1. Do you become more fatigued, tired or "worn out" by the end of the day?

2. Have you lost interest in your present work?

3. Have you lost ambition in your overall career?

4. Do you find yourself becoming easily bored (spending long hours with nothing significant to do)?

5. Do you find that you have become more pessimistic, critical or cynical of yourself or others?

6. Do you forget appointments, deadlines or activities and don't feel very concerned about it?

7. Do you spend more time alone, withdrawn from friends, family and work acquaintances?

8. Has any increase occurred in your general level of irritability, hostility or aggressiveness?

9. Has your sense of humor become less obvious to yourself or others?

10. Do you become sick more easily (flu, colds, pain problems)?

11. Do you experience headaches more than usual?

12. Do you suffer from gastrointestinal problems (stomach pains, chronic diarrhea or colitis)?

13. Do you wake up feeling extremely tired and exhausted most mornings?

14. Do you find that you deliberately try to avoid people you previously did not mind having around?

15. Has there been a lessening of your sexual drive?

16. Do you find that you now tend to treat people as "impersonal objectives," or with a fair degree of callousness?

17. Do you feel that you are not accomplishing anything worthwhile in your work, and that you are ineffective in making any changes?

18. Do you feel that you are not accomplishing anything worthwhile in your personal life or that you have lost spontaneity in your activities?

19. Do you find that you spend too much time each day thinking or worrying about your job, people, future or past?

20. Do you feel that you are at the "end of your tether"—that you are at the point of "breaking down" or "cracking up"?

The interpretation of any assessment tool is rarely foolproof or absolutely accurate. Your score on this test's inventory is merely a guide to understanding your experience of emotional exhaustion. The first step toward relief is the honest acknowledgment of your present condition. Biblical self-awareness is akin to personal revival. To recognize our total need of God for emotional well-being is to begin to comprehend the functional lifestyle of the deeper life. How did you score?

20-30 There is no emotional exhaustion. You may be taking your life or work too casually.

31-45 This is a normal score for anyone who works hard and seriously. Make sure you relax periodically.

46-60 You are experiencing some mild emotional exhaustion and could benefit from careful review of your lifestyle.

61-75 You are beginning to experience emotional exhaustion. Take steps to better control your life.

76-90 You are critically depleted emotionally. You should seek help, reevaluate your present life and make changes.

Over 90 Your present condition is threatening to your physical and mental well-being. Professional assessment is advisable.[4]

Mentors can help mentorees prevent exhaustion by asking, "What is your emotional state?" on a regular basis. For a more thorough and accurate assessment, mentorees can consult with their spouses or close friends. Check the test results with their intuitive and often uncanny accuracy.

Treatment and Development

The keys to developing a healthy emotional life and treating emotional exhaustion are similar:

1. Feed and regularly replenish yourself emotionally.
2. Limit your personal, emotional drains.
3. Discover what specifically feeds your emotions:
   - Music: nostalgia
   - Movies: help you feel, laugh, cry
   - Worship: your preferred style; both personal and corporate
   - Relationships: both friends and family
   - Support group
   - Some exercise
   - Journaling, listing, reflecting
   - A break, vacation, sabbatical or leave

Very specific attention needs to be given to addressing the emotional dimension of life and ministry. Feed both the emotional and the spiritual. Although we often make significant distinctions, they are more closely connected than most of us ever consider.

Feeding the Spiritual Side

Most of us in ministry have been given a pattern for spiritual development that goes something like this: "Read your Bible, pray every day, and you will grow." For many, a variation of that seems to work better than to

simply do one thing, the same thing, without any variation. As we practice the spiritual disciplines and their varied expressions, we often learn new ways to find intimacy
with God and to find refreshing for our spirits.

Mentors can give mentorees permission to take the
time to think through some new, innovative, even creative, ways of feeding the spiritual aspect of their lives.
A few years ago, I felt a particular need for some change
in my regular devotional pattern. I considered the fact
that I had memorized several hundred verses of Scripture and that I wanted and needed more exercise and
fresh air. So, I decided to take a three-month break
from my regular devotional pattern. I decided to do a
thirty-minute walk five mornings a week and to pick
five verses of Scripture every morning, taking time to
read over them. Then, as I walked I would run them
over in my mind, consider my life and see how true
those words were in the way that I lived. As I finished
my walk, I would come inside and do some additional
reflection and pray through ways in which I could incorporate those particular portions of God's truth into
my life in more significant ways. Although I did not
have classic, sit-down devotions that involved Bible
reading and prayer, those three months were some of
the best spiritual development that I have ever had.

I also discovered that as a pastor I had to give myself
permission to worship in different ways than those of
the church I pastored. At one point, when I was going
through a particularly difficult time, I felt like I needed
large doses of both emotional and spiritual input that I
found difficult to receive. I gave myself permission, and
also got permission from the chairman of my church

board, to do some different things. I was pastoring a mainstream evangelical church at the time, so I found an Anglican church that had a 7:40 a.m. service one town away. I could go into that small chapel, which had a tradition very unlike my own, meet with God, receive His mercy and grace and take communion weekly. I received both emotional and spiritual input in a very different style than I was accustomed to.

I also discovered during that time that I needed and enjoyed energetic worship, which was not the preferred style of the church I was pastoring, so I found another church to fill that need. Since we had a classic Sunday evening service that met at 6:00 and the Pentecostal church in town had a service at 7:30, I could leave our evening service in time to go to the other church and worship God there. For six months, I attended the neighboring churches, and during that time, I found that my experiences—both the quiet reflection at the Episcopal church and the more energetic and expressive Pentecostal service—did great things for me emotionally and spiritually.

Young leaders need permission to identify what they need and then figure out how to get it. A mentor can play an important role in talking this through and encouraging mentorees to intentionally feed and develop themselves emotionally and spiritually. Give yourself permission—and give other people permission as you are mentoring them—to try new things and explore new ways of connecting with God.

The Need for Balance

Having worked in an environment that has put me in contact with other people in ministry for the last fifteen years, I have discovered that the issues of emotional exhaustion and spiritual depletion seem to mostly affect two groups of people in ministry: men in midlife and single women. It often strikes single women because in our churches people are often not as considerate as they could be of the needs—particularly the emotional needs—of single people. As a result, there's a huge demand on many single people, particularly on women in ministry, without any corresponding emotional input.

> Young leaders need permission to identify what they need and then figure out how to get it. A mentor can play an important role in encouraging mentorees to intentionally feed and develop themselves.

The same thing seems to affect men in midlife. When their children were young, these men would come home and their children would wrestle with them or sit on their laps. There was a lot of attention, affection and intimacy. Then, when the men reached midlife and the children became teenagers, there was less affection and more conflict. The phrase that many men in midlife use is, "It feels as if everyone wants something from me that I don't have the energy or resources to give." Also, many of these men don't have close friends, and some will admit that there is not as much intimacy in their marriages as there once was. They are using up their energy without receiving any incoming support.

If we're going to help people in ministry to develop healthy patterns of emotional and spiritual development, it's imperative that in the mentoring relationship we give specific attention to learning to balance the emotional and spiritual aspects of life and ministry. We must learn to monitor ourselves and ensure that positive input is coming in so that we do not have leaders drained of their emotional and spiritual health.

Key Thoughts from This Chapter

1. It is imperative to not only check our physical and spiritual gauges, but also to understand how to keep our emotional tanks full.
2. Emotional exhaustion is the result of extensive emotional output without adequate emotional input. It is a sense that everyone wants something from you that you can't give.
3. We need to discover what feeds the emotional aspect of our lives and intentionally fill our emotional tanks consistently.
4. Young leaders need permission to try new things and explore new ways of connecting with God.

Questions for Further Reflection

1. Can you identify any ways in which emotional exhaustion may be an issue for you? What aspect of possible treatment interests you most?
2. How effective are you at reading your emotional gauge and recognizing when it is low? What are your symptoms and how responsive are you to this part of your life?
3. Is it time to give yourself (or someone else) permission to try new ways of connecting with God? What might that look like?

Action Plan

1. With a mentor, a spouse or a trusted friend, take some time to do an honest evaluation of your emotional and spiritual life. Begin to develop a plan for rebuilding your inner life resources.

Notes

1. Bill Hybels, "Reading Your Gauges," *Leadership*, Spring 1991, pp. 32-8.
2. Archibald Hart, "Psychology and the Kingdom," *Theology, News and Notes*, March 1994, p. 19.
3. Archibald Hart, "Pastor Burnout: An Introduction," *Theology, News and Notes,* March 1984, pp. 20-1.
3. Archibald Hart, "Red Flags of Emotional Exhaustion," *Leadership*, Spring 1987, p. 82.

11

Purpose, Passion, Plan and Priority in Mentoring

DON SIEBERT, A LIFELONG employee of J.C. Penney, started with the company working as a clerk, moved to managing a department and was promoted to managing a store. Ultimately, he became president and CEO of J.C. Penney at a time when innovation was needed to turn the corporation around. Don succeeded in doing this. He was a leader of leaders. He was a man who had a dramatic impact on the lives of many other women and men, both in the corporate world and in the Church. When he became president of J.C. Penney, he determined that one of his primary goals would be to begin grooming his successor. Although he was a relatively young man when he took the position, he knew that in order for the corporation to be successful in the long run, he needed to begin early on with grooming the person who would take over his position.

This is true in the corporate world, and it is true in places like the local church, the mission field and para-church organizations—everyplace where leaders are needed. One of the key roles of top-level leadership is to *intentionally* develop the next generation of leaders in order to keep the operation running successfully.

When developing a leader, there will be points along the way when the mentoring process needs to become quite focused. There will need to be some clear-cut directions established for determining how the mentoree will move into a new stage of development, how the relationship may take on a new dimension or how the mentoree will begin focusing on some new, specific aspects of leadership. For example, it may be time for the mentoree to move from the observing or planning role of leadership into the implementing or active phase. A purposeful intentionality will begin to emerge in the mentoring relationship because of this intensive focus on the relationship and its progression. It could occur early on in the mentoring process for some and much later for others. The role of the mentor remains much the same throughout the process: to be available, ask clarifying and evaluative questions and offer support, encouragement and assistance as needed.

Earlier, in chapter 2, I talked about a conference in Anaheim, California, at which I spoke about mentoring. As the conference concluded, we debriefed and received feedback from the participants, and the overwhelming response was that these leaders had focused on relational development and spiritual nurturing in their mentoring relationships, but they had done it without *intentionality*. As a matter of fact, the consensus was that intentionality was something many had avoided. They had not wanted to impose on the younger, emerging leaders. These more experienced leaders had been trying to mentor almost without anyone knowing that they were doing it. It was a shock and a surprise to them that the opposite would have been a positive approach.

Scripture shows us that adopting a *purposeful intentionality in producing leaders for ministry* can be highly effective. At many points throughout the Church's history, we've seen future leaders being molded by their leaders. Moses began early grooming his successor. Both Joshua and Caleb were chosen early in the Exodus to assist Moses in carrying out God's plan and purpose for the children of Israel. Jesus started developing His successors early as well. In Mark 1, He begins His ministry by calling the disciples to come and follow Him. In chapters 1 through 8, He is "with them," discipling, modeling and mentoring them. In chapter 8, immediately after Peter's confession, Mark states, "He then began to teach them that the Son of Man must suffer many things . . . and that he must be killed and after three days rise again" (8:31). After this, the tone of Mark's Gospel and Jesus' ministry change. He spends more time teaching, preparing and imparting His knowledge to the disciples. And finally, in chapter 16, He commissions them to go and reproduce this model to the ends of the earth. In both of these examples, the intentionality of starting early with developing future leaders resulted in success of bibilical proportions.

It is easy to hold up particular values or ministries as significant and valuable, but it is rather difficult to adjust your time, life and ministry priorities to successfully implement them. If mentoring and the development of emerging leaders is to be a reality in your ministry, it must be integrated into your ministry schedule with clear *intentionality*. Otherwise, it becomes another "good thing to do" or another "should" on the "to-do" list. Intentionality can be established through understanding the purpose of mentoring, clear planning, fixing priorities and adding your own passion to the mix. As a result, you will have a mentoring "soup," if you will, which combines all of the necessary ingredients to produce a conducive atmosphere for a successful, Jesus-style ministry.

Purpose

Over the past decade, many denominations have found it increasingly difficult to fill the senior pastor's position in larger churches. At times, dozens of candidates are interviewed unsuccessfully. The churches are often forced to go for long periods of time without a senior pastor, either utilizing a weekly pulpit supply or a long-term interim. Some have found it necessary to go outside the denomination to fill the position. Although every situation is different and there are a multitude of reasons for the apparent lack of suitable pastors, one key factor stands out: The next generation of pastors are not being mentored to lead the larger churches into effective ministry. Consequently, it is difficult for some churches to sustain their growth and effectiveness for more than two decades before decline—often significant decline—sets in. Mentoring a possible successor (or successors) should be done by every leader for the purpose of continuing the ministry and promoting its growth.

I do not want to single out leadership positions in larger churches only. Other leadership positions are also a challenge to fill. In developing the next generation of college presidents, seminary deans or presidents, and even the next president of a denomination, the intentional mentoring process could prove highly effective. In fact, many believe it should be the preferred model because it provides a structure for the emerging leaders to develop within and gives them exposure and experience they might not have otherwise.

However, there may exist a philosophical barrier for mentors in mentoring leaders for the next generation, especially for key leadership positions. We can sometimes be suspect of someone who aspires to such a position. We can have serious questions concerning that person's intentions and qualifications. Yet sometimes these may not be concerns at all. It is quite possible that the motivating factors for a young leader are a desire to serve, an inner calling and direction, the right personality and temperament or a specific passion. Women and men of God *do* have these internal motivating forces, and their desires can be quite pure and not carnal at all.

Ministry that emphasizes conversion, discipleship, spiritual nurture and development of the next generation of leaders should be the primary passions that the Church embraces and implements.

In the last two decades of the twentieth century, the Church has focused on numerous topics of life and faith in classrooms, seminars, sermons, literature, etc. The Church has also had its share of effective teachers, authors, preachers and leaders, both lay and pastoral—*but there are too few mentors to go around.* We almost need a mentor for every position available within a ministry organization. *The purpose of mentoring in ministry is to intentionally pass on key principles to the next generation in order to continue effective ministry.*

Passion

Figuring out your passion in life can be a difficult task. Ask yourself the following: "What are those things that clearly capture my imagination, that either push or drive me in healthy ways to participate for the greater good and that bring a sense of joy or fulfillment to me in the depths of my being? What are just one or two of those things?"

One strategy I have used in leaders' conferences in the last decade has been to ask people in ministry to compare their fantasies of ministry (back at a time when they were dreaming, philosophizing and fantasizing of ministry) with the present realities of their ministries. For some, it is a frustrating process; others talk about how little they knew would be involved. The common consensus that often emerges is that fantasies about ministry are *unrealistic* compared to the *reality* of ministry.

I then ask them to move away from the realistic terminology and focus on their fantasies. These are typically about life-change, people's lives and the gospel's power to see people dramatically converted and changed. Then I ask them to look at their motives both now and then, and the contrast becomes marked and sharp. I'll hear phrases such as, "I never had any idea that my motivation could be summarized by trying to keep people happy, to get through a board meeting or to make sure all the bases were covered." For many, running the organization, not getting fired and hoping people like them seemed to be a far cry from the original passions they had and the life-changing force of ministry they had dreamed of in the beginning.

One of the goals of mentoring is to provide an environment and a relationship in which mentorees are encouraged to dream dreams again. *Mentors will ask reflective questions and fan the flames of passion for ministry and the things that matter in life.* They will help mentorees to refocus, reprioritize and become centered again on what really matters, rather than have a perfunctory ministry.

As God dreams His dream for His Church, how do you suppose He desires the Church to spend its time? Clearly the life and ministry of Jesus indicates that the concepts of life-changing faith, personal development and conforming to the image of Christ are of high priority. So, ministry that emphasizes conversion, discipleship, spiritual nurture and development, equipping and the intentional development of the next generation of leaders should likewise be the primary passions that the Church embraces and implements. But accomplishing this mission requires adjustments to ministries, programming priorities and schedules. At the very core of a focused mission and ministry, a mentor will keep asking the reflective and evaluative questions that keep ministries and their leaders' lives in focus.

Plan

One of the primary emphases in leadership literature is the idea of conceptualizing a plan or vision and then working it through to completion. *Although the mentoring process is highly relational in nature, it is most effective when an intentional plan is developed and utilized.* When I do organizational consulting, the key question that I ask church and business board members is, "Why do you do what you do?" Sometimes the church and its leadership have not asked themselves this question for some time, nor do they have an answer. Sometimes the response is, "We do what we do because that is how we do it here, or how we have done it in the past." The old adage, "No one plans to fail; they just fail to plan," fits in these cases. Begin to create a plan.

> If each person would give ten percent of his or her time to the intentional development of other people, we could develop a healthy spiritual base for leaders in the Church.

Gary Kuhne, a discipleship guru in the 1970s, encouraged people to make sure that each meeting they had, no matter what kind or in what setting (discipleship, leadership development or mentoring), *had a purpose*.[1] Don't just meet for the sake of meeting or to feel good about getting together for a "worthy" cause or the sake of the ministry. Make sure that every meeting has a goal—particularly one that will develop the ministry, will enable a change in yourself or others or will nurture the growth of individuals. Let your passion for your ministry seep into your planning and touch every aspect of the meeting. Don't just think things will happen—you have to plan for them to happen.

Priority

In the last decade I have worked with several hundred pastors and leaders. Their ministries cover a wide range of experiences and levels of expertise. However, the evaluative questions I offer in each situation do not vary much. I ask them the following questions: How do you spend your time? What are the three most significant things you spend your time on? Is that the best way to spend your time? What is your primary mission? Do these areas in which you spend your time directly fulfill your mission? Is what you do necessary or just nice?

Conceptualizing, developing, keeping and working on your priority is an ongoing pattern of effective ministry. Note the ministry of Jesus in Mark's first chapter. He began His ministry by calling His disciples—a priority He kept throughout His entire ministry. Although He had an effective ministry in the community teaching, delivering and healing (1:21-34), He was willing to walk away from it all to keep focusing on those who had not yet heard the gospel. " 'Let us go somewhere else—to the nearby villages—so I can preach there also. That is why I have come.' So he traveled throughout Galilee, preaching" (1:38-39). Jesus' ministry was characterized by this kind of *priority*.

Developing a priority for ministry will consume your time, vision, thoughts, prayers and passions. Consider developing a ministry that includes the priorities of Jesus' ministry as they are set out in Mark 1: conversion, life-change, discipleship and leadership development. These are the essence of an intentional mentoring lifestyle.

A Tithe of Your Time

In the mid-'80s, I began to speak to pastors' groups across the United States and Canada about intentionally developing leaders. I began with principles of quality discipleship and spiritual nurturing and moved into intentional leadership development of existing leaders and, ultimately, the mentoring of others in ministry. The proposal I made to the pastors was as follows: If each person in a vocational ministry would give ten percent of his or her time to the intentional development of other people, in a matter of a few years we could develop a healthy spiritual and functional base for leaders in the Church. The ten percent would be *intentional* on their parts.

I explained that a forty-hour week of working in one's ministry translated into four hours of intentional discipleship, leadership development and mentoring. If a person worked for fifty hours, then five hours would be his or her tithe of time, and so on. This was a tithe of the first and the best ten percent of a person's time and priority. Then I asked them to project a bit, imagining the impact this would have on their churches in just a few years. I received positive responses. Pastors and lay leaders said, "I don't know why I haven't thought of this before." Many voiced strong commitments to incorporating this tithe into their lives.

I kept track of the pastors in the group who said they would follow through with this plan. I checked back with them periodically, sending letters, making phone calls and visiting their churches. Of the first 500 that I checked back with, less than 1 percent have actually followed through with the 10-percent tithe of their time in the 2-year period since our meeting. I heard many apologies, stories and even some excuses. But those who did follow through saw dynamic results.

As I mentioned in chapter 6, in many places around the world the Christian Church is growing stronger in numbers, and leadership development has become a focal point of missionaries' ministries. A significant number of them report that discipleship, leadership development and mentoring are a key part of their job descriptions, and, as such, the heart of how they spend their time and energy. If you look at the work of missionaries who are spending a significant portion of their time intentionally developing leaders versus the work of the average North American pastor who spends little time in this area, you can begin to see the significance and impact that intentional discipleship, leadership development and mentoring can make.

In a recent mentoring group of pastors from churches that are experiencing significant growth, a Hispanic pastor from Brooklyn talked about the uniqueness of his ministry. He said that the ministry seemed to work better when he intentionally developed the pastoral staff from within the congregation. He reflected, "I miss the interaction with the congregation, being their pastor, intimately involved in their lives. But now I spend sixty-five to seventy percent of my time in mentoring and leadership development. It seems necessary in order to continue and sustain the rate of growth we have experienced."

In most ministries, the way things have been done in the past establishes the pattern for the future. In order to break ineffective patterns, each leader will have to intentionally think through "Why do I do what I do?" and refocus his or her ministry on reproducing leaders. Commit to intentionally understanding the purpose and developing a passion, a working plan and a priority for mentoring the next generation of leaders. Imagine a tithe of your time, spent on a weekly basis, invested for the rest of your life in intentionally developing people in areas of spirit, character and passion for God and His work. Imagine how their lives could be different. Imagine how the Church could be different. Imagine how you could be different.

Key Thoughts from This Chapter

1. The key to mentoring is the *intentional* development of the next generation of leaders.
2. For mentoring to work in ministry, it is imperative to understand its purpose, fan the flames of passion for ministry, create a personal working plan and embrace it as a priority.
3. Develop a tithe of your time to intentionally focus on the next generation through discipleship, mentoring, spiritual formation, leadership development, etc. The future of the Church will be significantly impacted if you do.

Questions for Further Reflection

1. When you think about your successor or developing the next generation of effective leaders what people in your sphere of influence come to mind? In what ways are you already influencing them? How can you be more intentional in your influence?
2. How long has it been since you asked yourself, *Why do I do what I do?* Are you comfortable with the answers to your question? What adjustments need to be made at this time in order for you to be more effective?
3. Do you have the necessary tools (skills, confidence, etc.) to begin an intentional development of some next-generation leaders?

Action Plan

1. Rework your schedule and priorities so that a tithe of your time can be spent in intentional mentoring and leadership development.

Note

1. Gary W. Kuhne, *The Dynamics of Personal Follow Up: The Art of Making Disciples* (Grand Rapids: Zondervan, 1976), pp. 71-2.

12
Creating Working Formats for Mentoring in the Future

WHETHER OVER THE PHONE or over a cup of coffee at a conference, someone will inevitably ask me, "How can I find a mentor?" This question comes to me in various forms more than a hundred times a year. I've found that one of the keys in assisting people in the search for a mentor is to help them clarify their expectations, their perceived needs and their developmental and personal needs. Although there are subtle variations because of each person's uniqueness, the similarities of people's needs are overwhelming. Most people are looking for a guru, a spiritual giant, a sage or even the parent they never had. Having a mentor who fulfills only one of these roles will not result in a satisfied individual.

It is true that the mentoring relationship must consist of all the qualities mentioned thus far: listening, character, skills, asking questions, integrity, etc. Yet if we are to develop effective leaders for the future it will be necessary for the mentoree to rethink his personal expectations for his mentor and for the mentor to create alternative formats of mentoring. This chapter will explore the mentoree's expectations. It will also explore some alternative formats that mentors can use to structure various relationships to suit the mentoree's needs.

Expectations

In my first year as a seminary professor in Canada, I was in my early thirties and enjoying the teaching ministry very much. A colleague came to my office and asked if he could give me some wisdom. He affirmed to me that students found my teaching style appealing, and he said that he assumed that my style, when combined with my age and pastoral approach, would very soon bring to me dozens of students asking to be mentored or discipled. He commented on the long-term merits of such a relationship and then said, "Make sure you understand what each student is looking for. They will probably want at least one hour of one-on-one time per week. Most will want you to set the agenda. And depending on their particular needs or deprivations, they will want you to become their father, mother, pastor or friend, but especially the voice of God in their lives." He continued, "Just be sure that before you agree to something, you know what you are agreeing to. Be sure you both understand the other's expectations." His words have been extremely useful to me over the years.

Before beginning a mentoring relationship, it is important to consider the following questions: What are the expectations of both the mentor and the mentoree? Which party sets the agenda? What are the time frames for meeting? What will the outcomes of the meetings be? What format will be used for the meetings?

Assisting individuals in clarifying their needs is a critical beginning step in the process of developing leaders through mentoring. Sometimes it is as easy as simply asking them to explain their expectations, to describe how they see the process being beneficial and to state the outcomes they expect over a two-year period. Other times, it is necessary to probe a bit more to see what is behind the perceived desire or need for a mentor. You might need to determine if the person has a confidence issue, a security need, feelings of loneliness or a general feeling that he or she may be missing something. Others might have heard testimony from those who have profited in a mentoring relationship and simply assumed that they too needed a mentor. Establishing expectations and inner motivations for mentoring can aid the outcome in an effective mentoring relationship.

It is also useful to begin the mentoring relationship by identifying the resource people already present in the mentoree's life. Often, individuals search for a resource person "out there," when in reality they already know people who could serve as resources. The individuals simply have not learned how to utilize the wisdom, gifting and insight of the people who are already in their lives. Resource people can come from various places. They can be relatives and family members who pray with and for the mentoree, long-time friends who are at similar places in their personal and professional development or people at their place of work or in similar positions within the same organization or geographic location.

Another beneficial step in establishing the mentoring relationship is to ask potential mentorees to think beyond the idealized image of the mentor that may have already developed in their minds. Does the mentor have to be older, of the same gender, in a similar profession or from the same denomination, theological perspective or spiritual experience as the mentoree? Is it necessary for this be a one-to-one mentoring relationship?

A few years ago I served as a consultant for a large church in the northeastern United States. The church wanted to establish a mentoring program. Although the possibilities looked exciting and the outcomes could have been both powerful and diverse, we kept hitting a block. The leadership team believed that the mentoring program could only go forth in the traditional format. No matter what format, situation or model I presented, it was incomprehensible to them that the program could work in any form other than the traditional. Yet it is nearly impossible to create a church-based mentoring model that is one-to-one, older-to-younger and same-gender and effectively develop 300-500 people in 2 to 3 years! Much of the church's agenda could have been accomplished with some subtle variations—through small-group mentoring, peer mentoring and learning from people of wisdom, regardless of gender or age. That particular church needed only to open its mind to new mentoring possibilities to successfully reach its desired goal.

If we are willing to rethink the currently acceptable, traditional concept of mentoring, we can meet the current demand for mentoring relationships. As we have already discussed in previous chapters and seen from biblical models, there are many acceptable mentoring models that differ from the traditional—and work well.

Structures and Personal Style

Personal preferences can make a significant difference in how comfortable everyone in the mentoring relationship feels and how effective the relationship is. Different people have different preferences when it comes to structure, so the presence or absence of structure significantly affects the progress of the mentoring relationship. A mentoring agreement should be discussed and understood even in the most informal of settings so that expectations are clear to all involved.

Whether your preference is for a highly structured mentoring relationship or a loosely structured one, a few key guidelines should be addressed. These include:

1. The length of the relationship
2. The structures and details of proposed meetings
3. Boundaries
4. The degree of intentionality
5. The desired outcomes
6. Handling issues of confidentiality
7. Addressing difficult matters

Highly Structured Mentoring

Highly structured people like the mentoring relationship to have scheduled meeting times and a detailed agenda for each meeting, with assignments and materials to work through. The relationship will often include a variety of components: an agreement of expectations; a determined number of meetings with times set in advance; a list of possible assignments with established due dates; a list of probable issues to be addressed; a probable termination date; etc. Before beginning the relationship, both parties should clarify their expectations in order to resolve potential issues before they occur. State how you each see the relationship progressing in a structured way.

After spending eight years as a seminary professor, a consultant and a speaker, I thought it would be beneficial to my development to work through some professional issues with someone in my field who was more experienced than I. I prayerfully decided to contact one individual, and he agreed to enter a mentoring relationship with me. We decided to meet five times in the next year and a half since we would be attending the same conferences.

We turned out to be very different people. He was highly structured, an engineer type. His entire life was characterized by structure. Twenty years my senior, he had done well professionally, in ministry and relationally. In many ways it was a joy to be with him. But for everything he was, I was not. I was a product of the late '60s and early '70s. I liked freedom and flexibility. Discipline was not my great strength or preference. I preferred loose structures at best; no structures were better.

Establishing expectations and inner motivations can aid the outcome in an effective mentoring relationship.

It made for an interesting relationship. I joked with him at one point that we had a love-hate relationship (I loved him, and he didn't necessarily feel the same way toward me!). At the end of the year and a half, I had benefited greatly from this mentor. I didn't always like meeting with him, and at times I felt squeezed and pushed into a structured and controlled environment. But for me, the unique differences in our personal preferences made the experience useful. (I think I was helpful to him too, although he never admitted it!)

I learned that neither preference was good nor bad in and of itself; they were simply different avenues to accomplish the same goal. We debriefed about this on two occasions and concluded that our mission was the same and our ministries similar. God had used both of us beyond what we had dreamed; we just got there in very different ways.

Loosely Structured Mentoring

In loosely structured mentoring relationships, the same agreements should be set, the same guidelines established and the same outcomes discussed as in the highly structured setting. The most significant difference here is the detail to which these things are mapped out beforehand, the rigor with which the details are enforced and the flexibility with which they are adjusted along the way.

The Eagles Group, an intentional mentoring group that I began in 1996, has been a loosely structured group from its inception. It was organized along a structured set of guidelines, but these were not strictly enforced. Since the participants came from five states, set meeting times were established. A ten- to twelve-item agenda was sent to each member prior to the meetings. Assignments using sermon tapes, evangelism or small-group resources were distributed; a log of hours spent in ministry and a breakdown of how the time was spent were kept; and assessments and tests were taken and evaluated prior to meetings. All eight participants knew roughly what to expect before the meetings took place.

However, the group never determined in advance or even in a structured manner at the time of the meeting when items on the agenda would be discussed, who would take the lead on each item or how much time would be spent talking, sharing, teaching, praying, worshiping, etc. At the end of the session the group would look over the agenda and note that every item on the agenda had been addressed—but it was never clear when the transitions occurred from one item to the next. The facilitator (myself) was focused more on the development of the individuals and less on the content of the agenda.

Jack, a denominational leader in his thirties, heard about our group and asked if he could observe us. He wanted to see if any of the material could be reproduced cross-culturally, either for missionaries or for national leaders. The group agreed to allow him to observe, but only as a participant. Jack's greatest challenge became figuring out how to operate within our group's structures (or lack thereof). For the first meeting, I sent him a twelve-item agenda for a two-day meeting. He was impressed with the agenda and was anxious to see how we would cover all twelve items (especially knowing my style of leadership and the group's history).

I debriefed with Jack four times during the meetings. All of his questions centered around structure. He kept saying, "I don't know how you do it. We are accomplishing everything on the agenda in an in-depth way. I'm never quite sure which topic we're on, and I don't know when we move from one to the next. But I keep seeing the progression, and I sense the spirit of what's happening." During our final debriefing, he shook his head, saying, "Even though I've seen it, I can't believe it. We covered all of the items in depth. The relational aspect was highly significant and the life-change factor was dramatic. I felt the presence of God. It stirred the soul, developed the intellect and was productive on every level you said it would be. But it was so unstructured!" We discussed how important structures were—but that they were not primary, nor was the degree to which they were carried out. *Relationship* is significant. *Setting, atmosphere* and *context* are critical.

*****

Highly structured people can walk through the structures and get through their content, but at times they may have difficulty reaching the spirit of what's behind the structures. Loosely structured people can have a great time in relationship but often have difficulty accomplishing the mission or goal. The key is to create an established purpose. Create enough structure to accomplish that purpose, but always focus on the transformational aspect of personal, spiritual and character development.

Moving from his initial preference of a highly structured framework to a loosely structured one proved to be a welcome and beneficial challenge for Jack. Whatever structure you choose to implement, you will find that the emphasis placed on the relational context and the personal development of the individuals within the mentoring group are the keys to a highly effective outcome.

Types of Mentors

The Informal Mentor

Within the relational framework of mentoring is an ongoing developmental flow whereby a mentor can remain effective through various stages of the mentoree's life. The following are examples of the types of informal mentors a person can have throughout various stages of development.

Mentor: High school teacher and college choral director

Impact: Profound influence personally (ability to cope during brother's death and disintegration of family); confidence, reinforcement of personal values (contributing to society, making a difference, becoming a teacher, respect and regard for others, love of music); and, professional skills such as the ability to stand before a group to speak, write, etc. Very close relationship—surrogate parent.

Mentor: Trainer and boss

Impact: Trusted me to be able to handle any and all situations in administering the program in tandem or in his absence (in contrast, I had no confidence at all that I would know/be able to do what was needed); developed confidence in self and how to apply prior life and academic skills to present reality; learned that although there is magic to life, there is a minimum of mystery to working with people.

Mentor: Friend

Impact: Profound influence on personal skills which have professional application, e.g., openness to ability to communicate with others, other ways of knowing and perceiving the world and of processing information; ability to "read" multiple agendas in a meeting.[1]

Facilitated Mentoring

Facilitated mentoring is a structure and series of processes designed to create effective mentoring relationships, guide the desired behavior change of those involved, and evaluate the results for the protégés, the mentors, and the organization with the primary purpose of systematically developing the skills and leadership abilities of the less-experienced members of an organization.[2]

In her book *Beyond the Myths and Magic of Mentoring*, Margo Murray outlines a quality, "generic" mentoring model that is useful in a facilitated mentoring program and can be adapted to fit many varied professions and experiences.

In Murray's model, there are four keys in particular that help to make this a workable format, easily adapted to different people and preferences. First, there is consideration given to mentor-mentoree recruitment and selection. For Murray, the issue of who is selected for the mentoring process can determine much of the outcome: Is the mentoree ready for the next stage(s) of development? Is there a willingness and ability to make changes? Is this the right time in the mentoree's life for implementing changes? Second, there is *intentionality* of orientation and agreement negotiation. The significance of intentionality has been stated throughout this book, and Murray argues strongly for that intentionality to be spelled out in an agreement that can serve as a roadmap and a point of reference throughout the relationship. This leads us to her third key, which is the development and workings of an intentional plan. Finally, we see the specific culmination of the agreed-upon relationship and the evaluation of its effectiveness.[3]

These four steps are crucial in effective mentoring programs and relationships. This model can also be used in non-facilitated mentoring relationships as an adaptable format for both mentors and mentorees to consult throughout the relationship.

Peer Mentoring

Peer mentoring, although uniquely different from classical one-to-one, older-to-younger forms, can provide a highly beneficial experience for each member of the group. The concept has been a useful and well-received one in fields from education (with peer learning cohorts) to discipleship (with peer accountability groups). In many areas, the concept of peer groups developing together is an accepted part of the landscape. However, such has not been the case with mentoring—until now, where in some cases people have begun opening their minds to the possibilities of nontraditional formats.

In the late 1980s, Dr. Leighton Ford developed the Arrow Leadership Program for the purpose of intentionally developing younger (ages twenty-five through forty) Christian leaders around the world. One of the key components of the Arrow program is its peer mentoring groups. Each year, these groups are established in different ways. Some have been formed geographically, some by simply assigning people, some by affinity and yet others by gender.

As I went through this program myself, the peer mentoring group became one of the highlights for me. My group, consisting of myself and two others, had been formed geographically: We all lived within a 400-mile radius of each other. Our assignment was to meet together during the weeks we were at Arrow meetings (four one-week-long meetings within a sixteen-month period), and also in between these sessions at least once for personal prayer, accountability and mentoring. Although I graduated several years ago, my peer group still keeps in touch both by phone and in person. The relationships we formed were valuable, and we relied on each other for prayer, accountability and mentoring. We established a trust and a level of comfort that we can come back to at any time.

Those who are seeking a mentor but are struggling to find one should consider using the peer mentoring model. Within this model, members rely on each other for perspective. They listen, ask questions and seek spiritual guidance—all of the things you would seek in a "traditional" mentoring relationship. Yet, with the peer mentoring model, mentors do not necessarily have to be older or of the same gender. Often, the perspective offered by a group of mentors provides a multitude of perspectives that cannot be found in the one-to-one model. The following is a list of questions to use in a peer mentoring setting.

1. Describe your dreams when you fantasized about being in ministry.
2. How different is your ministry now versus the original dream? Which version of the ministry should you have?
3. Describe your personal goals for the next year.
4. Describe any fears or frustrations you face regularly.
5. What failures have you encountered in the last year or two and how did you respond to them?
6. Do you ever find yourself playing it safe out of fear of future failure? Describe it.
7. What do you do for fun? How regularly do you do it?

8. Describe your favorite leisure activity. How often do you incorporate it into your weekly schedule?

9. What does a typical "sabbath" look like for you? What are your regular practices of rest, relaxation, reflection and renewal? Describe them.

10. What sin(s) seem to come up in your prayer life for which you ask for forgiveness? Does it also need to be addressed in a manner other than confession? Identify the patterns of sin and confession in your life.

11. Is it difficult for you to receive forgiveness and "feel" forgiven?

12. What issues of lust do you face?

13. When you are tempted to abuse power, what does that look like for you?

Mentoring Across Genders

Early in my ministry, Mrs. Howard, a godly woman in her eighties, used to invite me to her home in the afternoons to pray. She was very nice about it, but her agenda was clear. It was obvious that, as a young pastor just starting out, I did not yet know how to pray. Mrs. Howard, in her kind but insistent way, felt that it was her responsibility to mentor me in prayer. She prayed with me, asked me questions and modeled prayer for me. Not only was it an acceptable form of cross-gender mentoring, but it was a highly desirable and effective one as well. Her gender in no way affected the effectiveness of her sharing her wisdom. She was simply a wise, older believer sharing her life lessons and knowledge with me.

In the context of the North American Church at the dawn of the twenty-first century, there are some crucial scenarios in which mentoring and teaching across genders is widely accepted. These are situations that involve prayer and insights into key biblical truths, wisdom and life. In each of these areas, the "teacher" is free to offer his or her experiences and insights.

> If we are willing to rethink the currently acceptable concept of mentoring, we can meet the current demand for mentoring relationships.

Another of my more recent experiences with cross-gender mentoring came during a week-long evangelism and leadership seminar at Dallas Theological Seminary. A group of thirty young leaders, both women and men, were directed by an insightful woman on the prayer life of a leader. As I sat in on this seminar, she recounted for the group how the Lord had been expanding her ministry of prayer. A whole section of her home had been given over specifically for prayer, and she felt the Lord opening up the ministry for her to pray with young women for their ministries. As she spoke, I felt very clearly that her mentoring would be useful for young men as well.

When she finished, the facilitator asked me to pray for her. I stood and said, "Is it possible that the Lord wants you to pray not only with young women but with young men as well? Isn't this a ministry you can pass across gender lines? Because there are so many young men in leadership who need coaching and mentoring in prayer. I think they would respond well to you." The group responded in consensus immediately, and she confirmed that day that this was clearly the Lord's direction for her. She continues to use her ministry across gender boundaries, effectively meeting young men as well as young women in prayer for their ministries.

Creating a Mentoring Plan

Regardless of the specifics of each mentoring situation, there are four guidelines to consider including in an effective mentoring framework. First, the relational aspect is foundational. This requires communication, time and risks. Second, asking questions and employing effective listening skills must be built into the relationship. Third, create agreed-upon guidelines and revisit them periodically. Finally, a mentoring format should have a built-in conclusion with an appropriate evaluation. These four guidelines will go a long way in keeping a mentoring relationship focused and effective.

*****

As we transition into the twenty-first century, a look back shows that much of the mentoring in ministry has been in preparation for a position within an organization or to become more functional at managing an established ministry program. However, as we stand on the edge of the future in the Church, the next generation of leaders are seeking developmental mentoring as a normative part of preparation for service and training. With that in mind, the exploration of various formats and structures for the mentoring relationship will significantly affect the process of intentionally developing the heart, character and spiritual formation and the necessary skills for the next generation of leaders to confidently take their place in the future ministry of the Church.

Key Thoughts from This Chapter

1. One of the key questions to answer up front in mentoring is, What are the expectations of those involved? Clarify expectations.
2. There are a variety of mentoring structures and styles:
   a. Highly structured mentoring
   b. Loosely structured mentoring
   c. Informal mentoring
   d. Facilitated mentoring
   e. Peer mentoring
   f. Cross-gender mentoring
3. Intentionally develop a working plan for mentoring and leadership development in your life and ministry.

Questions for Further Reflection

1. When you look at the various types of mentoring styles and structures, which has the most appeal to you? Can you adjust to a mentor or a mentoree who may have a different style? List two key adjustments you would need to make.
2. When you think of your mentoring expectations, what would be three to five key expectations for you as a mentor or mentoree?

3. Is mentoring and intentional leadership development another "should" for you, or can it become a clear purpose in your life? How do you begin to implement this mission?

Action Plan

1. Start where you are. Begin to pray for a clear plan for mentoring. Begin to identify those people with whom you would like to develop a mentoring relationship. Begin to adjust your schedule and life priorities to make it happen. Begin!

Notes

1. Karen D. Olsen, *The Mentor Teacher Role: Owners Manual*, 5th ed. (Oak Creek, AZ: Books for Educators, 1989), pp. 17-8.
2. Margo Murray with Marna A. Owen, *Beyond the Myths and Magic of Mentoring: How to Facilitate an Effective Mentoring Program* (Hoboken, NJ: Jossey-Bass, 1991), p. 68.
3. Ibid., p. 5.

Appendix 1:
Life Plan

IT'S BEEN CALLED "MIDLIFE crisis," "midlife reevaluation," "half-time," "moving from success to significance," "midcourse adjustment," "crunch-time" and many other things. When you reach a place in your life where it becomes clear either to you or to the people around you that it's time for you to do an assessment, *where do you start?*

This tool is designed for self-evaluation and reflection. You may want to have others assist you in the process. Realize that not every section will be the most pertinent for you, but seek to go through each of them in a thoughtful and reflective manner. This process may take you a few hours or, for some, a few days. It may cause you to reflect, find hope or maybe even shed tears. It is designed to assist you in more effectively evaluating the best of who you are and how to reach your dream in life.

Whether it's time for a change in lifestyle or career or simply a time for you to reevaluate how to do what you do more effectively and more efficiently, this life plan is designed to help you move from your original dream through the developmental stages of assessment to finally arrive at a future dream.

Original Dream

Describing your original dream takes you to a place of ultimate impact and fulfillment. It's a place where your life has maximum meaning. Almost everyone has a dream, but the fear of failure and concern about finances are often limitations. The purpose of this exercise is to help you figure out what it is that really captures your imagination, how you can be used the most and then how you can take steps to fulfill that original dream.

1. Go back to a time in your life—high school, college or some other time—when you were dreaming your original dream. Begin to define or describe that dream.
2. What really excites you about your original dream?
3. Do you possess the necessary resources—education, experience, discipline, courage, confidence, finances, etc.—to fulfill your dream? If not, can you secure them?
4. Do you think in terms of success in life or personal significance and influence? Do you think in terms of financial success or personal or spiritual impact?
5. How clear is your sense of a dream? Is it very undefined? Is there a general sense to it? Are there general steps for it to be accomplished?
6. What are two or three steps you could take to get you started on defining, discovering and fulfilling your original dream?

Your Gifts and Calling

Gifts/Passions

When you assess your areas of gifting, it's not just about reflecting on what you've done. It's also important to look at areas that you've not yet developed. Look at past successes and failures. Look at issues of confidence, or lack thereof, to see if they are holding you back. Also, look not only at your experiences, but also at your passion and your dreams. Then look at issues of your temperament, the time availability you have and your personal and spiritual maturity. This will help you figure out what your gifting and passion are and how you can best invest your life.

1. What do you like to do?
2. What have you been successful at?
3. What is a primary passion of your life? What do you dream about when you give yourself time and permission to dream?
4. Of the experiences you have had in the last five years, which ones have captured your imagination the most?
5. If you were guaranteed that success and money were not an issue, what would you do with your life?
6. Do you feel trapped, or is there fulfillment in what you do? Can you see yourself there for the long-term or even for the rest of your life?
7. When you look at how you are investing or have invested your time, energy and giftings, is this the best use of who you are? Is this as good as it gets for you?

Kingdom Investment of Your Life

It is important that, once you have discovered the particular gifts and abilities that God has given you, you examine whether you only use them to enjoy them or if you use them in ways that bring glory to Him.

1. Have you figured out how to take the best of who you are and invest it in God's kingdom in such a way that it reproduces dividends that last for an eternity?

2. Do you intentionally look for ways to take those gifts and abilities and use them in a way that other people can benefit from?

3. Are you confident in taking the best of what God has given you and using it as widely as possible, or do you simply use it in formats that are comfortable for you?

4. Do you see ways that God would like to use you that you don't feel confident doing now?

5. Are there times when you know that you're supposed to do something but don't have the courage or want to take the time to do it?

6. If you could be given one or two things that would help you take the best of who you are and invest it more completely, what would it be? Do you need courage, confidence, education, financial resources, empowerment or someone to walk you through the process? Do you need a mentor, friend or spiritual director? Do you need someone to pray with you and listen to you?

7. Think through any limitations that hold you back from investing the best of who you are. Begin to address those.

8. Interview several other people. Ask them ways they have seen God use you. Why did He use you in this way? Did it happen just once, or is there a pattern? Don't overlook old friends, members of churches you have attended, family members and ministers you have known. They can help you with this.

Calling: Clarification, Leading, Direction

There are three different types of calling. The first type is the general calling to be holy as God is holy and to love the Lord God with all your heart, soul, mind and strength. It's a general sense of leaving what you have to follow Christ completely. The second kind of call comes to specific people, such as the disciples of Jesus, who were called to leave their locations and their livelihoods to follow Him completely with their time and receive financial support for their sustenance. The third kind of call is a very specific one of which there are plenty of examples in the Bible: See the stories of Moses, Samson, Isaiah, Jeremiah, John the Baptist, Jesus and Saul of Tarsus. These individuals were singled out. They were often told that they had a purpose from before their birth. Their whole lives' purpose was to fulfill a particular destiny or calling that God had for them. Be careful about assuming that this third type of call is normative. It does still happen today, but if we only have a dozen or so examples recorded in the Bible, then we know that their occurrence is somewhat limited.

The key aspect of calling is *clarification*. Am I being called by God to follow Him with the totality of my life? Or is it also with the totality of my time, whereby I leave my current vocation and take on a ministerial vocation where I am paid by kingdom finances and resources?

A second aspect of calling is *leading*. One can have multiple leadings over his or her lifetime, all which will fit under some kind of vocational ministry. For example, I know a man who has been a pastor, a missionary, a supervisor of a thousand missionaries, a denominational executive, a college professor, dean and president and ultimately, president of a denomination. Those are not different callings, but rather different leadings under one calling.

A final aspect is *direction*. Direction is, "Where do I live this out? What are some concrete ways to live out my sense of calling and leading?" For example, if I am called to follow God completely and I am led to be a teacher, is God going to lead me in the direction of working with children, youth or adults? Is my work going to be spiritual development or also educational and academic development? Is it going to be at a college level or a graduate level? Is it going to be here in the United States or is it going to be overseas? Is it going to be in the urban core or is it going to be in suburbia or someplace in the heartland? As you look at your life, it is significant to clarify issues of calling, leading and direction.

1. Do you have a clear sense that God is leading you to resign from your career in order to use the full extent of your time and energies in serving Him?

2. If everyone is called to follow God completely, do you have a sense that He is asking you to follow Him with the totality of your life? Are you also convinced that you would do that

best by giving Him the totality of your time as well?

3. Do you have a sense that God wants you to stay in your career or location and continue to serve Him? Or are you to leave behind that career or location and receive financial support from kingdom monies in order to follow Him completely with your time as well as your life?

Your Career

There are a number of assessments that are helpful in determining a job or career. A popular book written to help in this area is *What Color Is Your Parachute?* by Nelson Bolles. A detailed career assessment tool called IDAK is also extremely useful in helping you discover for what career or job you are most suited. (An IDAK assessment will take you approximately eight to ten hours.) Ask yourself the following questions:

1. What do I fantasize about?
2. What is my dream job?
3. What will bring me the most fulfillment?
4. How do I invest my life in a way that it counts the most?
5. What are the outcomes of my life that I want to celebrate?
6. When I'm old and sitting on a porch in a rocking chair, looking back over my life, what do I want to have the greatest memories about?
7. When I near the end of my life, what will I wish I would have explored and gone for that I hesitated about and didn't pursue?
8. What can I do in life that brings me the greatest sense of accomplishment, fulfillment, satisfac-

tion and peace that also makes a difference in the kingdom?

Getting There

Intentionality

Looking at your life purpose and the intentionality with which you approach your life will really be the key to the fulfillment of your life plan. Begin to think in terms of how intentional and purposeful you are with your life, your giftedness and how you invest the best of yourself, your time and your resources each day. Look at your current situation and do some honest evaluation of where you are currently and how you arrived there.

1. How much of your life currently is a response to an intentional design or pattern of decision making?
2. Do you feel particularly directed by God to this situation?
3. Have you been systematically discipled?
4. Has your spiritual development been, or is it now, an intentional direction?
5. How intentional have you been with spending time with God? With key friends in your life? With developing relationships with family?
6. In your spiritual life, have you sought to replicate your giftedness, reproducing it in other people so they can benefit from it?
7. Is your current life purpose and vocation something that has grown out of thoughtfulness and intentional development, or have you just happened to stumble into what you're currently doing?

8. Do you thoughtfully dream and think about what your life is and could become or do you simply do what is required of you each day to get through it?

Other key questions to ask:

1. Have you participated in the intentional development of other people in your life?
2. Why did they choose you?
3. What did they see in you that they saw as either necessary or useful?
4. How did they impact you?
5. What's been their ongoing influence in your life?
6. How has that influence changed your life?
7. How have you or can you pass that on to other people?

Proper Motives

Some people do the right things for the wrong reasons. To discover why you do what you do, it is important to regularly check your motives. The following are some key questions to ask. Often nothing will show up. It is essential, however, that you do not try to answer these solely in your own mind, but that you have someone probe a bit into other aspects of why you do what you do. This should preferably be done with a mentor or an older, trusted friend with some wisdom who will ask you questions to clarify your purposes. A therapist's help may even be beneficial. It's important to note your idiosyncrasies here.

1. Why are you the way you are? What are the life experiences and decisions that have formed you as the person you are becoming?

2. Why do you do what you do? Why is it important to you? What are the key motivational factors for you?

3. What criteria have you used to make decisions?

4. Do you do what you do for the right reasons?

5. Who benefits the most from what you do?

6. Are there any improper motives that need to be checked?

7. Is there any way that you are trying to fulfill your life plan in such a way that it will ultimately hurt, harm, limit or even destroy you or someone else?

8. What are your temptations to do things that will make you look better in the public eye? Do you take too much responsibility for how well you did? Do you give credit where credit is due?

9. Do you have any "dark-side" temptations? Sexuality, addiction or addictive traits? (Again, to have a mentor, an older, wise friend or even a therapist help you with these regularly is helpful.)

10. Who asks you tough questions about your motives? Who speaks truth to you? Who is someone in your life who can tell you that you have made a wrong decision and to whom you will listen?

11. Do you have any patterns or tendencies to discredit people who do not agree with you? Do you discredit them as your opponents or do you take their advice and attempt to understand its implications for you?

Assessments help you create a personal profile of why you are the way you are and why you do the things you do. They will help you understand and see more objectively your preferences, the kind of person you are and God's work in your life and help you figure out how to develop from there. In choosing assessments, it is crucial to look at personality, temperament, preference, vocational contexts and leadership management styles. Here is a short list of recommended assessments and the area(s) they assess.

- 16PF: Personality profile
- Uniquely You: DISC profile, temperament analysis, spiritual gift assessment and summary profile
- IDAK: career assessment
- LEAD: leadership style
- Management Style Diagnostic Inventory: managerial style
- Networking: complete spiritual gift analysis and spiritual gift profile

Focus

There is the old adage: "Very few people in life plan to fail; they just fail to plan." This is a time to take a good look at your life and figure out what is holding you back and keeping you from fulfilling your life purpose. Ask yourself the following questions. You may also find it useful to pursue people in your life who will answer these questions for you.

1. How do you get a focus to your life?
2. What distractions in your life need to be addressed?

3. Are you a dabbler? Do you enjoy many things without focusing on one?

4. Do you have tendencies to overcommit and do more things than you can do well?

5. Are you aware of the things you do best? Are you confident in them? Do they bring you a sense of satisfaction?

6. What are clutter issues in your life? Timing? Relationships? Emotional or spiritual deprivation or needs?

7. If you were to ask the person closest to you, "What is the thing that keeps me from being successful or impacting others?" what would he or she highlight as the clutter that keeps you from experiencing success in your life?

8. What would that same person say was "good" in your life but was keeping you from doing your best?

9. How would the person who works closest with you but dislikes you answer the previous questions?

10. If you take stock in your life today, assuming that the current pattern will continue for the rest of your life, will you be happy with the outcomes?

11. Is this the time for you to get a clearer focus and rid your life of some "stuff"?

Areas to Develop

Don't forget that sometimes your greatest successes can become limitations. Sometimes you celebrate them too much and forget to keep a clear focus on priorities. Consider the three to five things in your life that you want to do most successfully and the values that drive you. Focus for a moment on any potential or perceived limitations to achieving your goal.

1. Do you take stock of your life in your emerging life plan?
2. What are the areas of your life that still need to be developed in order for you to fulfill this life dream, calling and life mission?
3. What areas need to be addressed with clear intentionality?
4. What areas of depth of wisdom, insight, relationship, spiritual understanding and understanding motivations need to be developed?
5. Is there anything holding you back?
6. Have you let a minor setback keep you from experimenting or trying something else?
7. Have you focused too much on one strength without pursuing additional strengths to accompany it?
8. Have you simply become accustomed to what you do? Although you are comfortable in your current situation, is it possible that it's not the best use of the totality of your strengths?
9. How do you maintain your passion?
10. How do you stay on the right road? How do you keep a clear focus and ensure that this isn't another tangent or another "to do" in your life, but really the purpose, direction and focus of your life?

After you have done this assessment for yourself, find some other people to help you. Utilize friends, family members, counselors, pastors, spiritual directors and pastors to ask you questions like:

1. What are some areas in my life that are yet to be developed?
2. What are the developmental steps needed for me to develop them?
3. How do I move from where I am to actually fulfilling my life plan?

Future Dreams

As you look at future dreams, ask yourself the following questions. All of these come together to create a life plan for you. The goal is to invest the life you have been given in such a way that it creates the greatest impact on the kingdom of God and in eternity.

1. What else is there for me?
2. Is there one more big challenge? Is there a mission or task that I need to undertake that I have not yet done?
3. Is there something that no one else is doing that I can do?
4. What maturity and development do I need in order to be able to do it?
5. Do I have a unique perspective, calling or purpose in life that could be used in ways I have not thought of? In ways that perhaps others have not thought of, either?
6. What will be the lasting impact of my life? How can I begin to plan for it now?
7. What resources do I need in order to fulfill my mission(s)? People resources? Financial resources? Educational resources? Experiential resources?

A lot has gone into making you the person you are now. Some things you have just assumed, a few you have regretted. But they have all gone into making you the person you are today. Attempt to see your life with the greatest outcomes in view, and also attempt to see your life from God's perspective. He does have a dream for your life. He is on your side. He is working with you to accomplish it. May your life fulfill both your dream and His for you.

Appendix 2:
Questions for Accountability[1]

1. Where are you at right now with God?
2. What have you read in the Bible in the last week?
3. What has God been saying to you in this?
4. Where do you find yourself resisting God these days?
5. What specific things do you find yourself praying for regarding others?
6. . . . for yourself?
7. What specific tasks are facing you that you consider incomplete?
8. What habits are intimidating you at present?
9. What have you read in the secular press this week?
10. What general reading have you been doing?
11. What have you done to play this week?
12. How are you doing with your spouse? Your kids?
13. If I were to ask your spouse about your state of mind, spirit, etc., what would she say?
14. Are you sensing any spiritual attacks from the enemy this week? Today?
15. If Satan were to try to invalidate you as a servant of God, where or how would he attack you?

16. What is the state of your sexual life (temptations, fantasy, etc.)?
17. Where are you at financially (Do you have control, debts, etc.)?
18. Are there any unresolved conflicts (ailing relatives, stress, disputes) in your circle of relationships right now (family, friends, those among whom we're supposed to feel safe)?
19. When was the last time you spent time with a friend of the same gender?
20. What kind of time have you spent with a non-Christian this past week?
21. What challenges do you expect to face in the coming month?
22. What are your fears at the present time (letting family down, bodies letting us down, etc.)?
23. Are you sleeping well?
24. What three things are you most thankful for?
25. Do you like yourself at this point in your pilgrimage?
26. What are your greatest confusions about your relationship with God?

Note

1. Taken from Gordon MacDonald, *Rebuilding Your Broken World*, as found in Gordon MacDonald, *Restoring Joy to Your Inner World* (New York: Inspiration Press, 1992), p. 573.

Appendix 3:
Suggested Resources

(*Alphabetical by Topic*)

Character

Alcorn, Randy. *Purity Principle: God's Safeguards for Life's Dangerous Trails*. Sisters, OR: Multnomah, 2004.

Bly, Robert. *A Little Book on the Human Shadow*. New York: HarperCollins, 1988.

Carter, Stephen L. *Integrity*. New York: HarperCollins, 1996.

Elmer, Duane. *Cross-Cultural Connections: Stepping Out and Fitting In Around the World*. Downers Grove, IL: InterVarsity Press, 2002.

Frye, John W. *Jesus the Pastor: Leading Others in the Character & Power of Christ*. Grand Rapids: Zondervan, 2000.

Ghent, Rick and Jim Childerston. *Purity and Passion: Authentic Male Sexuality*. Chicago: Moody Press, 1994.

Goffee, Robert and Gareth Jones. *The Character of a Corporation: How Your Company's Culture Can Make or Break Your Business*. New York: HarperBusiness, 1998.

Greer, Colin and Herbert Kohl, eds. *A Call to Character*. New York: HarperCollins, 1995.

Hendricks, Howard. *A Life of Integrity: 13 Outstanding Leaders Raise the Standard for Today's Christian Men*. Sisters, OR: Multnomah, 2003.

Hickman, Craig R. *Mind of a Manager, Soul of a Leader*. New York: John Wiley and Sons, 1992.

Hillman, James. *The Force of Character.* New York: Random House, 1999.

——. *The Soul's Code: In Search of Character and Calling.* New York: Warner Books, 1997.

Hybels, Bill. *Who You Are When No One's Looking: Choosing Consistency, Resisting Compromise.* Downers Grove, IL: InterVarsity Press, 1987.

Hybels, Bill and Rob Wilkins. *Descending into Greatness.* Grand Rapids: Zondervan, 1993.

MacDonald, Gordon. *The Life God Blesses: Weathering the Storms of Life That Threaten the Soul.* Nashville: Thomas Nelson, 1997.

——. *When Men Think Private Thoughts: Exploring the Issues That Captivate the Minds of Men.* Nashville: Thomas Nelson, 1996.

Nelson, Alan E. *Broken in the Right Place.* Nashville: Thomas Nelson, 1994.

Noonan, Peggy. *When Character Was King: A Story of Ronald Regan.* New York: Penguin, 2002.

Ogden, R. James, ed. *To Be a Person of Integrity.* Valley Forge, PA: Judson Press, 1975.

Pippert, Rebecca Manley. *A Heart Like His: Learning from David Through the Tough Choices of Life.* Downers Grove, IL: InterVarsity Press, 2002.

Smedes, Lewis B. *A Pretty Good Person: What It Takes to Live with Courage, Gratitude and Integrity.* New York: HarperPaperbacks, 1990.

Swindoll, Charles R. *The Quest for Character: Inspirational Thoughts for Becoming More Like Christ.* Portland: Multnomah, 1987.

Trent, John and Rick Hicks. *Seeking Solid Ground: Anchoring Your Life in Godly Character.* Colorado Springs: Focus on the Family Publishing, 1995.

Wiersbe, Warren W. *The Integrity Crisis.* Nashville: Thomas Nelson, 1988.

Coaching

Bandy, Thomas G. *Coaching Change: Breaking Down Resistance, Building Up Hope.* Nashville: Abingdon, 2000.

Blanchard, Ken and Don Shula. *Everyone's a Coach: Five Business Secrets for High-Performance Coaching.* Grand Rapids: Zondervan, 1995.

Brounstein, Marty. *Coaching & Mentoring for Dummies.* Foster City, CA: IDG Books Worldwide, 2000.

Collins, Gary R. *Christian Coaching: Helping Others Turn Potential Into Reality.* Colorado Springs: NavPress, 2001.

deLisser, Peter. *Be Your Own Executive Coach.* Worcester, MA: Chandler House Press, 1999.

Flaherty, James. *Coaching: Evoking Excellence in Others.* Boston: Butterworth-Heinemann, 1999.

Fournies, Ferdinand F. *Coaching for Improved Work Performance: How to Get Better Results from Your Employees!* Rev. ed. New York: McGraw-Hill, 2000.

Jerome, Paul J. *Coaching Through Effective Feedback.* Irvine, CA: Richard Chang Associates, 1994.

Lombardi, Vince. *Coaching for Teamwork: Winning Concepts for Business in the Twenty-First Century.* Bellevue, WA: Reinforcement Press, 1996.

Loritts, Crawford W., Jr. *Lessons From a Life Coach: You Are Created to Make a Difference.* Chicago: Moody Press, 2001.

Minor, Marianne. *Coaching and Counseling: A Practical Guide for Managers and Team Leaders.* Menlo Park, CA: Crisp Publications, 2002.

Parsloe, Eric and Monika Wray. *Coaching and Mentoring: Practical Methods to Improve Learning.* London: Kogan Page, 2000.

Developmental Issues

Buford, Bob. *Game Plan: Winning Strategies for the Second Half of Your Life*. Grand Rapids: Zondervan, 1997.

——. *Halftime: Changing Your Game Plan from Success to Significance*. Grand Rapids: Zondervan, 1997.

——. *Stuck in Halftime: Reinvesting Your One and Only Life*. Grand Rapids: Zondervan, 2001.

Miller, Patricia H. *Theories of Developmental Psychology*. New York: W.H. Freeman, 1993.

Robbins, Alexandra and Abby Wilner. *Quarterlife Crisis: The Unique Challenges of Life in Your Twenties*. New York: Jeremy P. Tarcher/Putnam, 2001.

Discipleship

Barclay, William. *Fishers of Men*. Philadelphia: Westminster John Knox Press, 1978.

Bonhoeffer, Dietrich. *The Cost of Discipleship*. New York: MacMillan, 1949.

Briscoe, Stuart. *Everyday Discipleship for Ordinary People*. Wheaton: Victor Books, 1988.

Bruce, A.B. *The Training of the Twelve: Timeless Principles for Leadership Development*. Grand Rapids: Kregel Publications, 2000.

Coleman, Robert E. *The Master Plan of Discipleship*. Old Tappan, NJ: Fleming H. Revell, 1987.

——. *The Master Plan of Evangelism*. Ada, MI: Fleming H. Revell, 1994.

——. *They Meet the Master: A Study Manual on the Personal Evangelism of Jesus*. Old Tappan, NJ: Fleming H. Revell, 1979.

Coppedge, Allan. *The Biblical Principles of Discipleship*. Nappanee, IN: Evangel Publishing House, 1989.

Fryling, Alice. *Disciplemakers' Handbook: Helping People Grow in Christ*. Downers Grove, IL: InterVarsity Press, 1989.

Green, Michael. *New Life, New Lifestyle*. North Pomfret, VT: Trafalgar Square Publishing, 1992.

Hadidian, Allen. *Successful Discipling*. Chicago: Moody Press, 1979.

Hauerwas, Stanley and William H. Willimon. *Resident Aliens: Life in the Christian Colony*. Nashville: Abingdon Press, 1989.

Hitt, Russell T. *How Christians Grow*. New York: Oxford University Press, 1979.

Hull, Bill. *The Disciple-Making Church*. Grand Rapids: Baker Book House, 1990.

———. *The Disciple-Making Pastor: The Key to Building Healthy Christians in Today's Church*. Old Tappan, NJ: Fleming H. Revell, 1999.

———. *Jesus Christ Disciplemaker*. Grand Rapids: Baker Book House, 2004.

Kinghorn, Kenneth C. *Dynamic Discipleship*. Grand Rapids: Baker Book House, 1973.

Kuhne, Gary W. *The Change Factor: The Risks and Joys*. Grand Rapids: Zondervan, 1986.

———. *The Dynamics of Discipleship Training: Being and Producing Spiritual Leaders*. Grand Rapids: Zondervan, 1978.

———. *The Dynamics of Personal Follow Up: The Art of Making Disciples*. Grand Rapids: Zondervan, 1976.

Murray, Andrew. *The Believer's New Covenant*. Minneapolis: Bethany House Publishers, 1984.

Pentecost, J. Dwight. *Design for Discipleship: Discovering God's Blueprint for the Christian Life*. Grand Rapids: Kregel Publications, 1996.

Peterson, Eugene H. *Run with the Horses: The Quest for Life at Its Best.* Downers Grove, IL: InterVarsity Press, 1983.

Stevens, R. Paul. *Disciplines of the Hungry Heart: Christians Living Seven Days a Week.* Wheaton: Harold Shaw, 1993.

Wagner, E. Glenn. *Escape From Church, Inc.: The Return of the Pastor-Shepherd.* Grand Rapids: Zondervan, 1999.

Emotional Development

Allender, Dan B. and Tremper Longman III. *The Cry of the Soul: How Our Emotions Reveal Our Deepest Questions About God.* Colorado Springs: Navpress, 1994.

Jakes, T.D. *Intimacy With God: The Spiritual Worship of the Believer.* Minneapolis: Bethany House, 2003.

May, Gerald G. *Care of Mind, Care of Spirit: A Psychiatrist Explores Spiritual Direction.* San Francisco: HarperSan-Francisco, 1992.

McDonald, Robert L. *Intimacy: Overcoming the Fear of Closeness.* Old Tappan, NJ: Chosen Books, 1988.

Miller, Stuart. *Men and Friendship.* Los Angeles: Jeremy P. Tarcher, 1983.

Nouwen, Henri J.M. *Intimacy.* San Francisco: HarperSan-Francisco, 1981.

Penner, Clifford L. and Joyce J. *Men and Sex: Discovering Greater Love, Passion, & Intimacy with Your Wife.* Nashville: Thomas Nelson, 1997.

Pittman, Frank. *Man Enough: Fathers, Sons, and the Search for Masculinity.* New York: G.P. Putnam's Sons, 1993.

Smedes, Lewis B. *Shame and Grace: Healing the Shame We Don't Deserve.* New York: HarperCollins, 1993.

Stoop, David A. and Stephen Arterburn. *The Angry Man: Why Does He Act That Way?* Dallas: Word, 1991.

Identity

Biehl, Bobb. *Why You Do What You Do: Answers to Your Most Puzzling Emotional Mysteries.* Nashville: Thomas Nelson, 1993.

Clinton, Tim and Gary Sibcy. *Attachments: Why You Love, Feel and Act the Way You Do.* Brentwood, TN: Integrity Publishers, 2002.

Trent, John. *Life Mapping.* Colorado Springs: Focus on the Family Publishing, 1994.

Intimacy

Allender, Dan B. and Tremper Longman. *Intimate Allies: Rediscovering God's Design for Marriage and Becoming Soul Mates for Life.* Wheaton: Tyndale House, 1999.

Benner, David G. *Sacred Companions: The Gift of Spiritual Friendship & Direction.* Downers Grove, IL: InterVarsity Press, 2002.

Dillow, Linda and Lorraine Pintus. *Intimate Issues: 21 Questions Christian Women Ask About Sex.* Colorado Springs: Waterbrook Press, 1999.

MacDonald, Gordon. *The Tests Men Face.* Brantford, Ontario: Women Alive, n.d. Audio recording.

Schaumburg, Harry W. *False Intimacy: Understanding the Struggle of Sexual Addiction.* Colorado Springs: NavPress, 1997.

Leadership Development

Batten, Joe, Gail Batten and Warren Howard. *The Leadership Principles of Jesus: Modern Parables of Achievement and Motivation.* Joplin, MO: College Press Publishing, 1997.

Beausay, William II. *The Leadership Genius of Jesus: Ancient Wisdom for Modern Business.* Nashville: Thomas Nelson, 1997.

Briner, Bob. *The Management Methods of Jesus: Ancient Wisdom for Modern Business.* Nashville: Thomas Nelson, 1996.

Briner, Bob and Ray Pritchard. *The Leadership Lessons of Jesus: Timeless Wisdom for Leaders in Today's World.* New York: Gramercy Books, 2001.

Clinton, J. Robert. *The Making of a Leader: Recognizing the Lessons and Stages of Leadership Development.* Colorado Springs: NavPress, 1988.

Cooper, Robert K. *The Other 90%: How to Unlock Your Vast Untapped Potential for Leadership & Life.* New York: Crown Business, 2001.

Donnithorne, Larry R. *The West Point Way of Leadership: From Learning Principled Leadership to Practicing It.* New York: Bantam Doubleday Audio Publishing, 1993. Audio recording.

Ford, Leighton. *Transforming Leadership: Jesus' Way of Creating Vision, Shaping Values & Empowering Change.* Downers Grove, IL: InterVarsity, 1991.

Goleman, Daniel. *Emotional Intelligence: Why It Can Matter More Than IQ.* New York: Bantam Books, 1995.

——. *Working with Emotional Intelligence.* New York: Bantam Books, 1998.

Harvey, Gareth. *Fast Track to Failure: A User's Guide to Abject Misery.* New York: HarperCollins, 1993.

Hayford, Jack. *The Leading Edge: Keys to Sharpen Your Effectiveness as a Leader.* Lake Mary, FL: Charisma House, 2001.

Lawrence, James. *Growing Leaders: Reflections on Leadership, Life and Jesus.* Elsfield, Oxford: The Bible Reading Fellowship, 2004.

Maxwell, John C. *The 21 Irrefutable Laws of Leadership: Follow Them and People Will Follow You.* Nashville: Thomas Nelson, 1998.

———. *Developing the Leader Within You.* Rev. ed. Nashville: Thomas Nelson, 2000.

———. *Developing the Leaders Around You: How to Help Others Reach Their Full Potential.* Rev. ed. Nashville: Thomas Nelson, 2003.

———. *Failing Forward: Turning Mistakes into Stepping Stones for Success.* Nashville: Thomas Nelson, 2004.

McCauley, Cynthia D., Russ S. Moxley and Ellen Van Velsor, eds. *The Center for Creative Leadership Handbook of Leadership Development.* San Francisco: Jossey-Bass, 2003.

McIntosh, Gary L. and Samuel D. Rima, Sr. *Overcoming the Dark Side of Leadership: The Paradox of Personal Dysfunction.* Grand Rapids: Baker Books, 1997.

Murdock, Mike. *The Leadership Secrets of Jesus.* Tulsa: Honor Books, 1996.

Parker, Russ. *Free to Fail.* London: Triangle, 1999.

Pearce, Terry. *Leading Out Loud: Inspiring Change Through Authentic Communication.* San Francisco: Jossey-Bass, 1995.

Rinehart, Stacy T. *Upside Down: The Paradox of Servant Leadership.* Colorado Springs: NavPress, 1998.

Roberts, Wess. *The Best Advice Ever for Leaders.* Kansas City, MO: Andrews McMeel Publishing, 2002.

———. *Leadership Secrets of Attila the Hun.* New York: Warner Books, 1990.

———. *Victory Secrets of Attila the Hun.* New York: Doubleday, 1993.

Sanders, J. Oswald. *Spiritual Leadership: Principles of Excellence for Every Believer*. Rev. ed. Chicago: Moody, 1994.

Segal, Jeanne. *Raising Your Emotional Intelligence: A Hands-On Program for Harnessing the Power of Your Instincts and Emotions*. New York: Henry Holt and Company, 1997.

Smith, Fred, Sr. *Leading With Integrity: Competence With Christian Character*. Minneapolis: Bethany House, 1999.

Stanley, Andy. *The Next Generation Leader: 5 Essentials for Those Who Will Shape the Future*. Sisters, OR: Multnomah, 2003.

Steinberg, Neil. *Complete & Utter Failure: A Celebration of Also-Rans, Runners-Up, Never-Weres & Total Flops*. New York: Bantam Dell, 1995.

Thrall, Bill, Bruce McNicol and Ken McElrath. *The Ascent of a Leader: How Ordinary Relationships Develop Extraordinary Character and Influence*. San Francisco: Jossey-Bass, 1999.

Timmer, John. *God of Weakness: How God Works Through the Weak Things of the World*. Grand Rapids: Zondervan, 1988.

Wilson, Earl D. and Sandy, Paul and Virginia Friesen and Larry and Nancy Paulson. *Restoring the Fallen: A Team Approach to Caring, Confronting & Reconciling*. Downers Grove, IL: InterVarsity Press, 1997.

Winebrenner, Jan and Debra Frazier. *When a Leader Falls: What Happens to Everyone Else?* Minneapolis: Bethany House, 1993.

Woolfe, Lorin. *The Bible on Leadership*. New York: Amacom, 2002.

Wright, Walter C. *Relational Leadership: A Biblical Model for Leadership Service*. Waynesboro, GA: Paternoster, 2000.

Listening

Hart, Thomas N. *The Art of Christian Listening*. New York: Paulist Press, 1980.

Murphy, Kevin J. *Effective Listening: How to Profit by Tuning into the Ideas and Suggestions of Others*. Salem, NH: ELI Press, 1992.

Robertson, Arthur K. and Robert B. Nelson. *Language of Effective Listening*. Carmel, IN: Scott Foresman Professional Books, 1991.

Men

Blitchington, Peter and Evelyn. *Understanding the Male Ego*. Nashville: Thomas Nelson, 1984.

Dalbey, Gordon. *Healing the Masculine Soul: How God Restores Men to Real Manhood*. Nashville: Thomas Nelson, 2003.

Eldredge, John W. *Wild at Heart: Discovering the Secret of a Man's Soul*. Nashville: Thomas Nelson, 2001.

Farrell, Warren. *Why Men Are the Way They Are*. New York: Berkley Publishing Group, 1988.

A Father's Legacy: Your Life Story in Your Own Words. Nashville: J. Countryman, 2000.

Hamrin, Robert D. *Great Dads: Building Loving Lasting Relationships with Your Kids*. Colorado Springs: Cook Communications, 2002.

Moore, Robert and Douglas Gillette. *King, Warrior, Magician, Lover: Rediscovering the Archetypes of the Mature Masculine*. New York: HarperSanFrancisco, 1990.

Morley, Patrick. *The Man in the Mirror: Solving the 24 Problems Men Face*. Grand Rapids: Zondervan, 2000.

———. *Seven Seasons of the Man in the Mirror*. Grand Rapids: Zondervan, 1995.

Smith, David W. *The Friendless American Male*. Ventura, CA: Regal Books, 1983.

——. *Men Without Friends: A Guide to Developing Lasting Relationships*. Nashville: Thomas Nelson, 1990.

Mentoring

Albom, Mitch. *Tuesdays with Morrie: An Old Man, a Young Man, and Life's Greatest Lesson*. New York: Doubleday, 1997.

Arrow Leadership Program: Mentor Training Seminar. Charlotte: Leighton Ford Ministries, 1996. Video.

Arrow Leadership Program Training Manual. Mentor training seminar. Charlotte: Leighton Ford Ministries, n.d.

Bell, Chip R. *Managers as Mentors: Building Partnerships for Learning*. San Francisco: Berrett-Koehler, 2002.

Biehl, Bobb. *Mentoring: Confidence in Finding a Mentor and Becoming One*. Nashville: Broadman and Holman, 1996.

Biehl, Bobb and Glen Urquhart. *Mentoring: How to Find a Mentor, How to Become One*. Laguna Niguel, CA: Masterplanning Group International, 1990. Audio recording.

Braden, Warren R. *Homies: Peer Mentoring Among African-American Males*. DeKalb, IL: LEPS Press, 1998.

Clinton, J. Robert and Richard W. Clinton. *The Mentor Handbook*. Altadena, CA: Barnabas Publishers, 1991.

Daloz, Laurent A. *Effective Teaching and Mentoring: Realizing the Transformational Power of Adult Learning Experiences*. New York: John Wiley and Sons, 1986.

Doyle, Mary K. *Mentoring Heroes: 52 Fabulous Women's Paths to Success and the Mentors Who Empowered Them*. Batavia, IL: 3E Press, 2000.

Engstrom, Ted W. *The Fine Art of Mentoring*. Brentwood, TN: Wolgemuth and Hyatt, 1989.

Gilley, Jerry W. and Nathaniel W. Boughton. *Stop Managing, Start Coaching! How Performance Coaching Can Enhance Commitment and Improve Productivity*. New York: McGraw-Hill, 1996.

Hendricks, Howard and William. *As Iron Sharpens Iron: Building Character In a Mentoring Relationship*. Chicago: Moody Press, 1999.

Hendricks, William, ed. *Coaching, Mentoring and Managing: Breakthrough Strategies to Solve Performance Problems and Build Winning Teams*. Franklin Lakes, NJ: Career Press, 2001.

Mallison, John. *Mentoring to Develop Disciples and Leaders*. Lidcombe, NSW, Australia: Scripture Union, 1998.

Murray, Margo with Marna A. Owen. *Beyond the Myths and Magic of Mentoring: How to Facilitate an Effective Mentoring Program*. Hoboken, NJ: Jossey-Bass, 1991.

Olsen, Karen D. *The Mentor Teacher Role: Owners Manual*. 5th ed. Oak Creek, AZ: Books for Educators, 1989.

Otto, Donna. *Finding a Mentor, Being a Mentor: Sharing Our Lives as Women of God*. Eugene, OR: Harvest House, 2001.

Peddy, Shirley. *The Art of Mentoring: Lead, Follow and Get Out of the Way*. Rev. and exp. ed. Houston: Bullion Books, 2001.

Phillips, Christopher. *Six Questions of Socrates: A Modern-Day Journey of Discovery Through World Philosophy*. New York: W.W. Norton, 2004.

Russert, Tim. *Big Russ and Me: Father and Son: Lessons of Life*. New York: Hyperion Press, 2004.

Schroeder, David E. *Follow Me: The Master's Plan for Men*. Grand Rapids: Baker Books, 1992.

Shea, Gordon F. *Mentoring: How to Develop Successful Mentor Behaviors*. Rev. ed. Menlo Park, CA: Crisp Publications, 2001.

Sinetar, Marsha. *The Mentor's Spirit: Life Lessons on Leadership and the Art of Encouragement.* New York: St. Martin's Press, 1998.

Southard, Betty. *The Mentor Quest: Practical Ways to Find the Guidance You Need.* Ann Arbor: Servant Publications, 2002.

Stanley, Paul D. and J. Robert Clinton. *Connecting: The Mentoring Relationships You Need to Succeed in Life.* Colorado Springs: NavPress, 1992.

Taylor, Andrea S. and Jeanette Bressler. *Mentoring Across Generations: Partnerships for Positive Youth Development.* New York: Kluwer Academic/Plenum Publishers, 2000.

White, Joe and Jim Weidmann, eds. *Parents' Guide to the Spiritual Mentoring of Teens: Building Your Child's Faith Through the Adolescent Years.* Wheaton, IL: Tyndale House, 2001.

Zachary, Lois J. *The Mentor's Guide: Facilitating Effective Learning Relationships.* San Francisco: Jossey-Bass, 2000.

Questions

Biehl, Bobb. *The Question Book.* Nashville: Thomas Nelson, 1993.

Leeds, Dorothy. *Smart Questions: The Essential Strategy for Successful Managers.* New York: Penguin Putnam, 2000.

Mains, David and Melissa Mains Timberlake. *Getting Beyond "How Are You?": Learning to Connect in a Disconnected World.* Wheaton, IL: Victor Books, 1992.

Osterhaus, James. *Questions Couples Ask Behind Closed Doors: A Christian Counselor Explores the Most Common Conflicts of Marriage.* Wheaton, IL: Tyndale House, 1996.

Smart, Bradford D. *The Smart Interviewer: Tools and Techniques for Hiring the Best.* New York: John Wiley & Sons, 1989.

Stock, Gregory. *The Book of Questions*. New York: Workman Publishing, 1985.

———. *The Book of Questions: Business, Politics, and Ethics*. New York: Workman Publishing, 1991.

———. *The Book of Questions: Love and Sex*. New York: Workman Publishing, 1989.

Women

Arterburn, Stephen and Fred Stoeker. *Every Woman's Desire: Every Man's Guide to Winning the Heart of a Woman*. Colorado Springs: Waterbrook Press, 2001.

Dillow, Linda. *Creative Counterpart: Becoming the Woman, Wife, and Mother You've Longed to Be*. Nashville: Thomas Nelson, 2003.

Farrel, Pam. *Woman of Influence: Ten Traits of Those Who Want to Make a Difference*. Downers Grove, IL: InterVarsity Press, 1996.

Hubbard, M. Gay. *Women: The Misunderstood Majority: Overcoming Myths That Hold Women Back*. Nashville: W Publishing Group, 1992.

Hunt, Susan. *Spiritual Mothering: The Titus 2 Model for Women Mentoring Women*. Wheaton, IL: Crossway Books, 2004.

Kraft, Vickie. *Women Mentoring Women: Ways to Start, Maintain, and Expand a Biblical Women's Ministry*. Rev. ed. Chicago: Moody Press, 2003.

Roberts, Cokie. *Founding Mothers: The Women Who Raised Our Nation*. New York: HarperCollins, 2004.